"I'm always in awe of Morgan Daimler's ability to draw together often complex ideas and to make them accessible without losing the essence of them, and this book is no exception. It combines the thorough academic research we expect from Morgan and Morgan's personal experience to introduce this fascinating, and sometimes misunderstood goddess. If you're looking to get to know Macha, you really need to start here".

Icy Sedgwick, host of the Fabulous Folklore podcast

What People Are Saying About

Macha

It is not often that Macha is recognized as the powerful enigmatic goddess she is in her own right. *Macha – Meeting the Great Queen of Ulster* is an excellent scholarly deep dive into her lore and associations. It will serve as an invaluable resource for modern practitioners who wish to deepen their understanding of this powerful goddess.
Stephanie Woodfield, author of *Priestess of the Morrigan*

Macha – Meeting the Great Queen of Ulster by Morgan Daimler is a long overdue exploration of a goddess frequently mentioned in modern paganism but rarely understood. From the complex literary sources for Macha, the possible origins of the name itself, her appearance in various tales and her significance as part of the Morrigan lore, a fascinating picture emerges of a deity that is important and autonomous in her own right. Morgan leads the reader through the available material, combining impeccable scholarship with her usual accessible and interesting style. She examines each story, each version of Macha, with care building up to a coherent overview. An added bonus is the author's own interpretation of this goddess and generous insights into her relationship with Macha and guide to connecting with Macha in the modern word. If you are interested in An Morrigan, and the relationship between Badb, Morrigan and Macha, this is an invaluable book, whether you're familiar with Irish pantheon or a complete newcomer. If you want to develop a relationship with Macha, I would go so far as to say this is an essential read.
Geraldine Moorkens Byrne, author of *Draíocht Ceoil, The Sound of Magic in Irish Traditions*

For anyone interested to learn more about Macha, whether just getting to know this powerful deity or wanting to delve deeper into a personal connection with her, Morgan Daimler's book is the best resource. Starting with the first mentions about Macha in the Old Irish manuscripts and progressing into a modern-day perspective of her, Morgan Daimler takes the reader on a journey to uncover the many aspects of this goddess. The book gives thorough consideration to academic viewpoints, archaeological findings and lore while beautifully weaving in the author's personal gnosis. Great scholarship and personal style blend syncretically in *Macha,* a book which stands out as both a homage to the goddess and a guide for those seeking her.
Daniela Simina, author of *Where Fairies Meet: Parallels between Irish and Romanian Fairy Traditions*

One Morrigan or three? One Macha or five? Morgan Daimler takes those questions head on in her new book for *Macha – Meeting the Great Queen of Ulster*. What I like about Daimler's presentation is that she gives enough information for the reader to decide. She also takes the position that these Machas and Morrigans are iterations of the same Goddess. Daimler does both with honesty and scholarship. This book is the most thorough treatment of our pagan connection to Macha that I have found. It is refreshing to have the loose ends gathered together, because Goddess knows Irish myth can be confusing to the outsider. Daimler has made herself an insider by reading old texts in the original, consistently honoring the Goddess, and walking the Land. I finished this book about Macha the Irish Goddess understanding the Macha I know better than before. I highly recommend meeting the Goddess of Ulster by reading *Meeting the Great Queen of Ulster* by Morgan Daimler.
Dorothy Abrams, author of *Identity and the Quartered Circle*

Pagan Portals

Macha

Meeting the Great Queen of Ulster

Pagan Portals

Macha

Meeting the Great Queen of Ulster

Morgan Daimler

MOON BOOKS

London, UK

Washington, DC, USA

CollectiveInk

First published by Moon Books, 2026
Moon Books is an imprint of Collective Ink Ltd.,
Unit 11, Shepperton House, 89 Shepperton Road, London, N1 3DF
office@collectiveinkbooks.com
www.collectiveinkbooks.com
www.moon-books.net

For distributor details and how to order please visit the 'Ordering' section on our website.

ISBN: 978 1 80341 962 6
978 1 917991 28 5 (ebook)
Library of Congress Control Number: 2025942875

A CIP catalogue record for this book is available from the British Library.

Design: Lapiz Digital Services

UK: Printed and bound by CPI Group (UK) Ltd, Croydon, CR0 4YY
US: Printed and bound by Thomson-Shore, 7300 West Joy Road, Dexter, MI 48130

The manufacturer's authorised representative in the EU for product safety is:
eucomply OÜ - Pärnu mnt 139b-14, 11317 Tallinn, Estonia, hello@eucompliancepartner.com, www.eucompliancepartner.com

This book is dedicated to everyone who looks to Macha
and anyone who is seeking her.

Huge thanks to everyone who offered suggestions for
Macha in fiction/tv/games including:
C Lee Vermeers, Josh Heath, Helen Compton,
Mark Fitzgerald, Leo Stewart, Cynth A B Salas,
and Laurel Ronan

No generative AI was used in any
way for any part of this book.

All material was written by the author or
quoted from a human written source.

Contents

Author's Note

This book in many ways is very different from my other Pagan Portals, as it was written across nine months as part of a Work In Progress blog project through Moon Books website, and is structured differently from my usual approach. However, with Macha I think this structure works better and I hope readers will find this book easy to navigate. Macha is a goddess who is very close to my heart and I want this book to be the perfect introduction to her for those who don't know her and hopefully also offer something to those who do. I have also included a variety of my own personal experiences here, which I think help to illustrate the active side of connecting to this powerful deity.

I personally favour using APA citation in my writing and so throughout this book when a source is being cited you will see the name of the author and date of the book in parenthesis after that. This indicates the book that is being paraphrased in that sentence, both for clarity and to allow readers to further research for themselves if they choose to. I have also included endnotes expanding on points that don't fit neatly into the larger text but are important to touch on, as well as a selection of resources in Appendix B.

The intention of this book, as with all my Pagan Portals, isn't to offer a definitive or exhaustive guide to this goddess but rather offer a solid introduction which covers all the most essential aspects of Macha and her mythology. While ideally even experienced people will still find something in here to pique their interest or will learn something new, the point of this short work is an introduction not a dissertation. So, take it in the spirit it is intended, and consider Appendix B and the bibliography if you want to go deeper.

Beannachatí na trí Morrignae duit.

Introduction

> *"Mythology is the stuff of continuity, not consistency, and the inconsistencies apparent throughout Morrigan lore may well be artifacts of that very continuity."*
>
> – Angelique Gulermovich Epstein

This work is personal for me, an exploration of a deity that I have honoured for decades and who inspired me to begin writing nonfiction and to take risks on my own spiritual path. I have written about Macha before, but only in bits and pieces, each focused on one particular thing or one story. Here for the first time all of my research and all of my love for Macha will be pulled together and expanded to offer others both a historic and personal look at her, from our oldest sources to today. I hope that readers will appreciate the blend of both fact and personal thoughts, and will find this work useful in their own explorations of Macha, as we dive past the surface material into the layers of her stories, archaeology of her sacred site at Emhain Macha, pre-Christian Irish culture, and the wider views of her found now.

Many people think of the Morrigan when they hear Macha's name, as she is widely understood to be one of the three Morrigans, but not as many may understand that Macha was a powerful being in her own right. RAS MacAlister, a 20th century Irish archaeologist, suggested in his notes on Volume 4 of the *Lebor Gabala Erenn* that originally the Morrigan and Badb formed a divine duo and it was only later that Macha, the main goddess of Ulster, was added in and the duo became a trio. This idea is supported by looking at both place names and stories which suggest that Macha was a dominant figure in Ulster, particularly around Armagh – Ard Macha, literally Macha's Height – while Badb was well known in the northwest and the Morrigan in central Ireland. Over time the three war goddesses came to be connected and eventually understood as three sisters who often acted together. However, even then Macha remained somewhat autonomous, not appearing with the other two as often as they appeared together and having a place within stories without them.

I have always been a believer in the importance of looking at the etymology and meaning of names to gain a better understanding of the being. This is true of Macha as well, because her name can show us a layer to her that is often ignored or overlooked. The word macha in older Irish means a milking field or yard, a place where cows are milked; in modern Irish it has lost the milking connation but is still used for a cattle field generally and also for a herd of cows. It is important to understand in context that cows have historically played a huge role in Irish culture, representing both sustenance as well as wealth. For an example of this, a cumal[1] was a term for an amount of value, generally understood as three milk cows or 35 acres of land, while another term of value, sét, represented ½ a milk cow (eDIL, 2024). Cows were units of currency, the value further set by the type and age of the cow, and so wealth and social status hinged on cows as well (Sherwood, 2009). The meaning of macha and the word's connection to milk cows would have indicated that the goddess's name was intrinsically connected to those same concepts.

Macha is an intriguing but also complex figure and one who is often misunderstood today. To begin, even deciding which stories Macha is in is more difficult than one might expect. There are five different appearances of figures named Macha across Irish myth and it is unclear whether these five are identical or merely share a name. This is further complicated by the already convoluted and often contradictory genealogies we have for the Irish Gods and the fluid nature of both myth and belief. Each iteration of Macha is said to die within their stories, and yet death never stops an Irish deity from reappearing later, sometimes again within the same story, so even this doesn't necessarily preclude one Macha who reappears in different contexts. On the other hand, it isn't uncommon for beings with the same name to be clearly different individuals who simply share a common name. MacCana describes Macha explicitly as an Irish war goddess, but avoids discussing Macha of the Tuatha De Danann/the Morrigan, instead focusing on Macha the wife of Nemed, Macha Mong Ruadh, and Macha the Fairy Woman, suggesting that each of those represent versions of a single sovereignty goddess. Toner adds Macha of the Tuatha De Danann as a fourth option but argues that Macha the Fairy Woman and Macha wife of Nemed are later literary inventions, in contrast to the more genuine Macha Mong Ruadh and Macha of the Tuatha De who are associated with war. Ó'hÓgáin chooses to focus primarily on only two Machas, Mong Ruadh and the Fairy Woman, while simultaneously declaring Macha another name for the Morrigan, rather than one of the three. Waddell points out, echoing MacCana, these various myths do not contradict each other but instead complement each other and offer confirmation of details (Waddell, 2014). In particular we can see connections between Macha wife of Nemed, Macha Mongruadh, and Macha of the Sidhe who are all listed together in a single entry in the *Dindshenchas* and who all strongly convey themes of fertility and creation (Sjoestedt, 2000). Indeed, within the three distinct Machas can be seen a single warrior figure who is linked by her name to the land itself; we may also relate these three to the three functions of Dumezil's tripterate theory as they fill the roles of sacredness, warriorship, and fertility respectively (Waddell, 2014). In the same way they each relate to a different class of people based on Dumezil's theory, with Macha the Nemedian being of the priestly class, Macha Mongruadh of the warriors, and Macha of the Sí of the producers. There is a certain continuity between their stories which all feature Macha as a figure associated with the concept of creation and also with the building, clearing, or naming of a physical location. Additionally, we can see that each aspect of Macha, including Macha of the three Morrigans, has ties to the nobility or elite, and each of their stories shows Macha influencing either a king, who is ruling as king, or the security of the land itself, reaffirming her ties as a sovereignty Goddess. That all said, however, there is no wide consensus about Macha in academia, only a range of theories and opinions. Whatever view someone may have about these five Machas and their connections – or lack thereof – can be as easily supported as contradicted leaving it open to each individual to decide how they feel about the topic.

For myself, I tend to treat all five as versions or iterations of the same being. I think that to understand any particular Macha one needs to look at all of them, to see the patterns between the stories and study the differences. I am acknowledging that bias upfront, but will strive to present the information as neutrally as possible so that everyone can draw their own conclusions. One of the most beautiful things about this goddess, in my opinion, is her complexity and the way that everyone understands her slightly differently; there is no single 'correct' way to understand her but rather a multitude of possibilities.

This book will look at each appearance of Macha across mythology, with the first five chapters looking at one particular Macha, the sources we have for her, her story, and what we might learn from this. It will be for the reader to decide if these five are all the same being or not, as that is something even academics disagree on. Each chapter will also include a discussion of a related subject that adds context to understanding Macha in that story, so that, for example, Chapter 4, Macha of the Sidhe, will also look at beliefs around the Tuatha De Danann and Aos Sidhe and the connection to fairy beliefs. By understanding the cultural context and some of the deeper symbolism of the stories we can come to a deeper understanding of Macha herself. Further chapters will dig into Macha's symbols and associations, how to connect to her, common misunderstandings around her, and ways that she has and does appear in the modern world. Each chapter will also include a short section at the end called 'Macha in My Life' where I will relate a personal story of my own experience with the goddess. Ideally a reader will see the complexity around Macha and the ways that her themes and purviews weave across the various stories into a cohesive whole, so that the confusion can be removed.

Macha was, and still is, the pre-eminent goddess of Ulster, a figure who represents the sovereignty of the land as well as the power of battle, justice, magic, and prophecy. Each face of Macha, each appearance within a tale, reveals another piece of who she is and what she can do, and within *Pagan Portals – Macha* we will explore as much of this material as possible, introducing readers to this goddess or perhaps offering a deeper understanding for those already familiar with her.

Chapter 1

Macha Daughter of Partholón

"The names of the ten noble daughters
whom Partholon had....
Aife, Aine, lofty Adnad,
Macha, Mucha, Meleprad,
Glas and Grenach,
Auach and Achanach."

– Lebor Gabala Erenn (Macalister, 1944)

The first Macha we will be looking at is also one who we know almost nothing about. She is barely a note within a wider story, yet she still represents the first time the name Macha appears in Irish myth. According to the *Lebor Gabala Erenn* Ireland was invaded or settled five consecutive times by different groups: first by Cessair, then Partholón, the Fir Bolg, the Tuatha De Danann, and finally by the Gaels. It is during the second settlement that we first hear of Macha who arrives with her father, Partholón, and his people.

The Story

The first settlers of Ireland were a woman named Cessair and her people which included forty-nine women and three men; all but one would eventually drown when Ireland was flooded by the Biblical deluge. This interweaving of Irish mythology with Christian myth is common and reflects the scribes attempts to reconcile the Irish myths with their own Christian cosmology. The only survivor was a man named Fintan who transformed into a salmon and lived in the water; later he would take the form of an eagle and a hawk before returning much later to a human form.

Ireland remained empty after that for 300 years until the arrival of Partholón and his people, including 10 daughters and three or four sons, as well as around 9,000 others. The people of Partholón settled Ireland and introduced civilization to the island, including farming, and fought the first battle ever on those shores, against the Fomorians.[2] However, after several years a plague came, arriving on Bealtaine/1 May, and wiped out all of Partholón's people within a week, leaving Ireland uninhabited once again.

In this myth we find Macha listed as one of the 10 daughters of Partholón along with two other names found among the Tuatha De Danann later: Áine and Aoife. It is perhaps interesting to note the meanings of the names of these women, beyond Macha which was discussed in the introduction: Áine – brightness, Aoife – beauty, Adnad – kindling, illuminating, Mucha – early morning, Glas – green/blue/grey, Grenach – boisterous. Meleprad, Auach, and Achanach are uncertain. Macha is also named as a druid among the people of Partholón (O'Donovan, 1848)

This Macha is a mystery, a name within a list of names, and so we can say little about her with certainty. But we can take a wider look at the people she came with and their accomplishments to make some tentative assumptions about her. The Partholónians arrived in an Ireland that was nearly untouched by humanoid beings,[3] a wild and untamed place. Macha and her people began changing that, reshaping the land and according to the *Lebor Gabala Erenn* while Ireland had only consisted of one plain, three lakes and nine rivers previously during the time that Partholón's people were there seven new lakes appeared and four plains were cleared; this is likely symbolic of the arrival of civilization to the island. This may be supported by a later passage of the text which claims that it was these people who first built a house, 'put a cauldron over fire', brewed beer, and prayed in Ireland. This Macha then is associated with the first people to not only begin changing Ireland from wilderness to settlement but also to introduce comforts beyond survival. It is also possible that the terraforming in the story may reflect much older ideas of a creation tale that has now been lost, as creating plains and rivers can have cosmogenic significance – literally creating and shaping the world or place being described.

This leaves us with Macha of the Partholónians as a figure associated via her kin with creation, land shaping, and bringing civilization and the skills associated with it. As a druid she would also have been someone who mediated between her people and the gods of her people.

Sources for Irish Mythology

As we move further into the stories of Macha, I think it's helpful to offer a basic overview of the sources we have for Irish mythology and what exactly we are working with. It has long been my own approach to start by looking at primary sources and so, especially in these first few chapters, we will be relying mainly on these texts. In later chapters we will cover more recent folklore as well and that is a different well to draw from. I've also found that there is a lot of confusion about what sources we do have so hopefully this can help clarify for people and make it easier for readers to go out and find more material on their own.

So, what are we actually working with? While you may sometimes see people claiming that we have little to no older Irish material, it's more complicated than that. We do in fact have a wide range of manuscript sources, with the older sources dating to the 5th century. Where it gets tricky, however, is that we don't have anything that was written by the pre-Christian Irish – everything we have was recorded and preserved by Christian monks or scribes. This has created one of the most pervasive divides in the study of this material: Nativism which sees all preserved material as containing some degree of genuinely Irish material, and Anti-Nativism which sees all existing material as influenced by and reflecting foreign texts. It is perhaps also important to keep in mind that conversion in Ireland didn't happen quickly but was a process that spanned centuries. The early Irish law texts, which date to the 7th and 8th centuries, include references to Druids and their honour price, that is how much would be owed to them for various injuries, as well as what legal maintenance they were owed, which indicates that even 200 and 300 years after Christianity established itself in Ireland some vestiges of paganism remained. This overlaps with the earliest manuscripts, meaning that stories started to be recorded when there was still some degree of pagan presence. If we trace various figures through the texts, we can see the slow change in the material into the 17th century when it is overtly Christian and pagan material has been reduced to spectres and demons or literary characters.

If we were seeking purely and entirely pre-Christian Irish beliefs then we have none, but if we are willing to accept that there is material from the early Christian through medieval period that still holds a lot of pagan beliefs then we have a great deal to work with. I choose to hold the latter view.

We are also not dealing with a static or fixed body of material. We have some very old stories that have survived in manuscripts as well as more recent material with clear evolutions in belief evident. We have regional variations which place one figure as the main actor in a place where that figure was primarily acknowledged and then another version elsewhere that gives the same role to a different figure. We have the stories written in manuscripts and we have later folk tales and folk beliefs. Irish mythology is a beautiful and complex tapestry formed from all of these things, interwoven with newer ideas and personal theories.

Here are also some key points that should be kept in mind:

1. All translations are not made equal and translations often lose a lot in the translating. Many people approach translations of older material as if they represent exactly what the older sources said but it's best to let go of that idea. Translations are always less nuanced than the original and may have implications in English that don't exist in the original language. There are also issues with Victorian era translators adding or removing material based on their own feelings and beliefs, so that, for example, Whitley Stokes omitted an important section of the *Cath Maige Tuired* based on his feeling that it was too obscene for his audience. It is always best to treat a translation as a close estimate of the original and not to read too much into any particular text or piece of information based on what a translation says.
2. Older mythology isn't the same as modern retellings of stories or of modern folklore. The oldest myths exist in a fixed written form and we can point to the texts we have as sources for certain ideas or stories. Modern retellings often offer these same stories but with various differences, including streamlining the tale, combining different older textual versions into a single source, or adding the author's personal ideas and opinions. In the same way newer folk beliefs reflect a variety of sources that may have influenced the story from euhemerization to local details. None of these sources are necessarily better or worse than others but it is important to understand the differences between them. Many things that are repeated now as 'ancient Irish belief' actually originate in the 1980s or 1990s outside Irish culture and many things that are found in older Irish material have become obscure.

3. We don't have any single cohesive version of any Irish myths or stories in the manuscripts[4] with the possible exception of the *Cath Maige Tuired* which only exists today in one text. What we do have are a range of manuscripts from the 9th century onwards which can vary greatly in details based on where and when they were written, who wrote them, and what wider cultural factors were going on at that time. This gives us in many cases a variety of stories which exist in different versions which may have significantly different details – for example, in one version of the *Táin Bó Cúailgne* it is Badb who warns the Donn Cúailgne, contests with Cu Chulainn and so on while in others it is the Morrigan who does these things. For another example, the famous encounter between the Morrigan and Cu Chulainn where she appears in disguise as a princess, is found in only a single version of the *Táin Bó Cúailgne*; in all others that episode isn't present.
4. Older stories must be understood in the context of the cultures they come from. For example, it's difficult to really understand the meaning of Macha's name without having the context of the value of cows within Irish society, because that value is intrinsic to understanding the importance of a milking field. In the same way some older Irish myths like the *Oidheadh Chlainn Tuireann* reflect the political landscape of Ireland at the time the story was written down, giving us two very different stories of how the Tuatha De Danann overthrew the Fomorians – in the *Cath Maige Tuired* the battle began when the Tuatha De, en masse, rose up against the Fomorians who were oppressing them, while in the later *Oidheadh Chlainn Tuireann*, written when Ireland was under Norse oppression itself, describes a beaten down people who have to be forced to rise up by an outside agitator in the form of Lugh. Nuada in the *Cath Maige Tuired* is a

noble king who lost his throne when he lost his arm but is willing to fight for his people, while the Nuada of the later story is a weak-willed king unwilling to fight.

5. A final point – Irish mythology is still evolving. We tend to think of mythology as historic material, and the bulk of what we have is older. But these are still living beliefs and they continue to evolve across the older myths and into modern living folk belief. We see this in the way the Lugh of mythology became the Lugh of folk belief, or the way Áine went from one of the Tuatha De Danann to a fairy queen to a human woman but all while retaining a place in folk belief. Irish culture is alive, Irish story telling is alive, and so the stories themselves are fluid and adaptable. We can (and should in my opinion) be clear about what is or isn't older belief or recorded myth but we also have to be aware of modern concepts and ideas within the living culture that include mythic concepts and beings.

Ultimately, we can say with some certainty if an idea is older or newer, if it is an Irish folk belief or coming from popculture, but we need to understand the range of sources and how they work together. And in looking at who Macha is we should look across as many of these sources as possible, using them like puzzle pieces to slowly create a cohesive image of her.

Macha in My Life – Meeting the Goddess

The first time I remember learning of Macha is when I was in my early teens. I am sure I knew of her before that, if only in a vague way, but when I was around 13 or 14, I went to the Metropolitan Museum of Art in New York City with my friend Éilís and her mother. In the gift shop there was a small section of books on 'Celtic' mythology and I was excited to get a copy of one which included retellings of popular myths. In it I found the tale of Macha racing the king's horses[5] and I was immediately intrigued. There was something about the idea of a goddess who interacted so closely with humans, who understood human pain, and who enacted justice that seemed designed to create empathy that appealed to me. Unfortunately, this was the early to mid-1990's so the information I had access to was often distorted or outright wrong; I had to alter my understanding of who and what Macha was several times across the next decade, until I started to find better sources to look at, and eventually was able to access stories in original translations instead of retellings. My understanding of Her has changed a lot over the years but that core first impression remains.

No matter how my wider understanding of who and what Macha is may have evolved over time, that core love for her which began when I first read the story of Macha racing the king's horses has always remained.

Chapter 2

Macha of the Nemedians

"Eva, Cera, praiseworthy Medar, gentle Macha, a lovable company like to assured peaceful rest, were the women of Nemed the strong."

– Banshenchus

In Chapter 1 we explored Macha of the Partholónians and discussed the *Lebor Gabala Erenn* which suggest that Ireland was settled in waves by various primordial beings before finally being inhabited by humans. Here we must also mention another group of beings who feature across Irish mythology: the Fomorians. These chthonic beings are given no clear backstory or origin but appear first during the time of Nemed (discussed below) as frightening and powerful raiders who exert their influence on those who settle Ireland. Some scholars suggest the name Fomorian might mean 'under the sea'[6] and the term has been connected to the idea of sea pirates or raiders. The *Cath Maige Tuired* suggests they are the people of the sidhe, perhaps existing there before the Tuatha De Danann arrived, although other sources contradict this idea. They are described in most ways as being very similar to the other groups which settle Ireland like the Tuatha De Danann, and while never explicitly called gods, it is implied they have similar powers, although this is usually described as being rather monstrous in nature. They often embody greed and excess in stories they appear in and are almost always the antagonists in tales which include them. And as you shall see as we proceed into the story of Macha of the Nemedians, they are powerful adversaries.

The Story

After the plague wiped out the Partholónians, Ireland was empty for about 30 years until the Nemedians arrived. They were led by Nemed, whose name is a word in older Irish which means a sacred place, privilege, or sacred thing; it was also a term used for a high-status person within society. Nemed's four sons came with him as chieftains and they and all of his people settled the land, creating four lakes and 12[7] plains and building two forts (Macalister1941; Gwynn, 1924). Macha is named as the wife of Nemed, and it is said that she was the first to die of his people in Ireland, 12 years after they landed.[8] In the *Lebor Gabala Erenn* her husband cleared the land to create the plains but in an alternate version of the story she clears the land and then has a prophetic vision of the death and destruction of the future *Táin Bó Cúailgne* which causes her to die of a broken heart (Green, 1992). According to the *Edinburgh Dindshenchas* it was after Nemed cleared the twelfth plain, which would be named for her, that she dreamt of the Táin and the evil which would occur during it and died. She was buried at Ard Macha [Macha's height] which was named for her, and one of the plains that the Nemedians cleared was also named for her, Mag Macha. The *Dindshenchas* call her '*lovely*' while the *Banshenchus*, quoted above, calls her gentle (Gwynn, 1924).

During his lifetime Nemed fought and won three battles against the Fomorians, who sought to oppress his people, but afterwards died of sickness, as the plague which had consumed the Partholónians seemed to have still haunted the new settlers of Ireland, although not quite as devastatingly. This unfortunately left his people open to Fomorian influence and they soon fell under heavy taxation by two Fomorian warriors, where they were required to give 2/3rds of their children, crops, and milk to the Fomorians every Samhain.[9] This tax weighed heavily on the Nemedians, or as the *Lebor Gabala Erenn* more poetically puts it:

"Wrath and sadness seized on the men of Ireland for the burden of the tax" (Macalister, 1941).

In rebellion the Nemedians raised an army of 60,000, half fighting on land, the other half on the sea, to attack those who were oppressing them. They overthrew and killed one of the Fomorians but the other rallied his own forces and destroyed all but 30 of the Nemedians. One of Nemed's sons, Ibath [Death] and his son went to the north (often a metaphor for the Otherworld) while another of Nemed's son's went to settle Britain and several grandsons to Scotland, and finally Nemed's son, Semeon, went to Greece. In this way the few survivors dispersed and went on to establish their own nations, leaving Ireland uninhabited again.

Who Were the Nemedians?

Of the various groups who settled Ireland the Nemedians are one of the most pivotal, if not the most pivotal. This may surprise some people who would immediately assume that the Tuatha De Danann would be more important but without the Nemedians the subsequent settlements wouldn't have been possible, because they are the progenitors of both the next two groups who settled in Ireland. The Fir Bolg were the eventual descendants of Nemed's son, Semeon, while the Tuatha de Danann were the descendants of Nemed's son, Ibath. The Nemedians laid the groundwork for these later returns both literally by continuing the process of civilization of the land in Ireland and figuratively by establishing Ireland as a homeland for their descendants to return to.

It is important to understand these stories, but also to look at the metaphoric layers, to see Nemed as representing the sacred and sacred people who established a home – who made Ireland a sacred space – and were driven out by the Fomorians, representing chthonic and entropic forces, only to later reclaim Ireland with waves of returning descendants, one group of which are considered the Gods of Ireland. While Cessair and Partholón began the process of making Ireland habitable, or in some views creating it, Nemed blessed it, and was the hinge that turned the narratives from establishing to active tales.

Macha of the Nemedians

As with Macha of the Partholónians, Macha of the Nemedians is a somewhat mysterious figure. She is barely referenced in the story, and then only as the wife of Nemed and the namesake of a height and plain. We may, of course, extrapolate that she was the mother of Nemed's sons, which isn't given explicitly but is a logical assumption, and therefore ultimately one of the ancestors of the people who would eventually be formed by those sons, including the inhabitants of England and Scotland, as well as the mythic groups of the Fir Bolg and Tuatha De Danann. It is interesting as well to note that Macha is referred to as one of the druids of Partholón and then appears next among the Nemedians who have intrinsic connections to sacredness. This then may show us an aspect of Macha that is part of these things, a Macha who embodies the sacred and brings that energy into new places.

It may seem confusing here to talk about Macha as a being who appears and dies only to reappear in another story, and as mentioned in the introduction not everyone believes that each of these Machas are the same being. But it's also worth noting that Irish gods dying and popping back up apparently alive and well again isn't that strange and occurs in a range of stories; the best example may be Miach who is killed early in the *Cath Maige Tuired* only to reappear shortly thereafter – clearly as the same being – working to help heal injured warriors. Death isn't ever really permanent for the gods. It may also appear strange that Macha might be her own ancestor or descendant but again this seems to be an aspect of Irish pagan belief[10] and is something we see in other stories. For example, Cu Chulainn is the son of the god Lugh but is also, often simultaneously, thought to be a reincarnation or avatar of Lugh by many people. The Irish gods exist both within and beyond our understanding and manifest in a range of ways throughout the myths that are sometimes difficult for us to fully comprehend.

Pseudohistory and Mythic Figures

Something we run across quite frequently in Irish myths is an attempt to tie the stories and characters into either Biblical narratives or human history, or both. This euhemerization is widespread in older pagan stories which were recorded by Christians and it's very important to understand this framework for what it is and not to get too caught up in trying to prove the history of myths or to understand the gods as previously human beings. The Christian scribes were working from a cosmology that denied the existence of other deities and so sought to explain these beings as historic humans, often from foreign cultures. There was also an attempt to tie Irish stories to Biblical narratives to show their value and connect Ireland to the Christian world, hence Cessair was connected to Noah and the flood of Genesis and many genealogies of Irish gods are traced back to Biblical figures. In the same way the scribes tried to establish that the figures of Irish myth, particularly the various groups which settled the island, had ties to the classical world which established their importance, wider value, and connected them to human history as it had been recorded in Rome. Through this approach the *Lebor Gabala Erenn* claims the Nemedians are descendants of Noah, who Nemed's lineage is traced back to, and came from Scythia; in contrast the *Historia Brittonum* says they came from Iberia (Macalister, 1941; Giles, 2000). Neither of these should be taken entirely at face value as historic truth but should be interpreted within the context of scribes trying to anchor these tales within their own cosmology.

In Irish mythology it is also common to see some real-world concepts or places used metaphorically rather than literally. The north, for example, is often referenced in places where the Otherworld is meant, with north being strongly connected to the Good Folk who are called 'tuaith geinte' [northward-moving folk] in some older sources. In the same way antagonistic or dangerous beings and groups are often associated with Norway or the Vikings, symbolizing threat. Again, these aren't literal descriptions or associations but are being used in ways people in the culture of the original texts would have understood on a metaphoric level.

When reading the myths and trying to connect to Macha it's important to keep all of this in mind, and to see the layers that exist within the stories, and to try to avoid falling into either tunnel vision or an overly literal interpretation.

Macha in My Life – Macha in Difficult Times

Macha is a complex deity, as we are exploring in this book, and one who has a range of facets to her: she is a goddess of prophecy and abundance as much as she is of war and battle magic. She is a creator of sacredness and sacred space. To me she has also been a goddess who is ideal to turn to in difficult times, both practically and spiritually. Her stories as often as not are messy, and for every time we see her triumph we can find another time she failed; I find this very relatable and also very hopeful. If a goddess can suffer and fail and keep striving then so can I.

When I have faced challenges in my life it is usually Macha that I turn to. In 2006 when I started feeling pulled away from the Irish focused path I'd been following for 15 years (at that point) it was Macha I looked to, to help me find my way in uncharted territory. When I almost died in 2012 from anaphylaxis and then again in 2013 from post-birth complications it was Macha who gave me strength to keep pushing forward. I always felt as if she was there with me, in some sense, encouraging me not to give up. I found that every trial I went through in life helped me understand her stories better and gave me a deeper insight into who she was and is. I found her in my own struggles as much as in dusty histories, and I could see some small piece of myself in her tales.

Chapter 3

Macha of the Tuatha De Danann

"It was then that Badb and Macha and the Morrigan went to the Knoll of the Taking of the Hostages, and to the Hill of Summoning of Hosts at Tara, and sent forth magic showers of sorcery and compact clouds of mist and a furious rain of fire, with a downpour of red blood from the air on the warriors' heads; and they allowed the Fir Bolg neither rest nor stay for three days and nights."

– The First Battle of Moytura

The Story – the Cét-Cath Maige Tuired and the Cath Maige Tuired

After the Nemedians were driven from Ireland the island was once again abandoned, this time for 200 years, until one group of their descendants, the Fir Bolg, returned and settled there. After establishing themselves and ruling for 30 years, however, the king of the Fir Bolg had a dream that a flock of blackbirds flew to Ireland and overwhelmed his people and this was interpreted by the king's druid as a dream foretelling the arrival of the Tuatha De,[11] which came to pass.

After spending the intervening years studying magic, the Tuatha De Danann returned to Ireland in ships which flew through the air and landed on a mountain, bringing darkness and mist for three days.[12] They engaged with the Fir Bolg peacefully at first, asking for room to settle alongside them in Ireland but the Fir Bolg refused; in response the Tuatha De challenged the Fir Bolg to a battle to see who would get to remain on the island. Macha initially appears along with her two sisters, who go to the seat of kingship in Ireland, Teamhair [Tara], and use their magic to subdue the Fir Bolg for three days. Later the two groups meet at midsummer to fight: the first day the Fir Bolg win and the Tuatha De are soundly pushed back. The second day we are told that the Morrigan, Badb, Macha, and Danann[13] accompany the leaders of the Tuatha De to the battlefield and the day's fighting results in a draw. The third and final day of fighting the Morrigan, Badb, and Macha along with their three sisters Fotla, Banba, and Eriu and their two foster mothers Be Chuille and Danann go with the warriors to the front lines and raise a series of stone pillars in the field[14] to keep their forces from retreating. Although the king of the Tuatha de Danann loses his arm in the fighting the Tuatha De are victorious, killing most of the Fir Bolg and driving the remaining warriors into Connacht.

Because the king, Nuada, had lost his arm he could no longer continue ruling so in his place the people chose Eochaid Bres, the son of a Tuatha De woman and Fir Bolg father, to be the next king. Although Bres was described as incomparably beautiful, he wasn't a good king, withholding hospitality from his people and allowing his paternal kin to tax them terribly. Because of this, and because Nuada's arm was healed, after seven years the Tuatha De Danann demanded that Bres step down as king. He initially agreed but asked for a delay before doing so and used this time to go to his father's people and raise an army to subdue the Tuatha De and take the kingship back by force. The Tuatha De Danann rallied behind Lugh, who like Bres was half Fomorian and half Tuatha De although it was Lugh's father who was among the Tuatha, in part because Lugh was skilled in all arts and in part because he had been prophesied to kill his grandfather, the Fomorian King Balor. After much preparation the two groups finally confronted each other at Samhain[15] and the Tuatha De emerged victorious; according to the story Nuada and Macha fell together at the hands of Balor before Lugh killed him.

This offers a short version of the combined tales of the first and second battles of Moytura, the main pivotal myths of the Tuatha De Danann. Although Macha doesn't feature prominently, she does play an important role in the first story, and the second offers us insight into her death, impermanent as such things are for the Gods. In the first battle we learn that Macha is a sorceress among her people, as she goes with her sisters and works battle magic against their enemies. She also appears accompanying the warriors to the fight on the second and third days of engagement, although it is unclear whether she fights with them or is merely there to offer support; in contrast in the battle against the Fomorians we are told that Macha falls along with Nuada in the fight and while we aren't explicitly told she was fighting alongside him it is certainly implied.

We also find Macha referenced in other stories of the Tuatha De Danann in ways that give us further insight into who she is in this context, although she is most often mentioned in conjunction with her sisters Badb and the Morrigan. While these pieces of material lack wider context and story, they nonetheless provide a deeper view of who Macha of the Tuatha De is. With that in mind I'd like to explore the main ones I have found:

Lebor Gabala Erenn – Macha is listed in this text as a daughter of Ernmas and sister to Ernmas's other children including Badb, the Morrigan, Fotla, Banba, and Eriu. Along with her two sisters Badb and the Morrigan she is said to be a source of '*bitter fighting*' and '*a well of craftiness*' (Macalister, 1941).

The *Banshenchus* – The *Banshenchus* is a poetic list of various female characters in Irish myth which includes some small details about them. In this text Macha is listed along with Nemain, Danann, Badb, the Morrigan, Etain, and Be Chuille who are all described as witches of the Tuatha De Danann. It is interesting to note that all of these except Nemain and Etain are the same women who accompany the men to the battle with the Fir Bolg in the *Cét-Cath Maige Tuired,* indicating that perhaps in that story they were there for magical battle support.

The Glossaries – The Irsan text (MS 1337 Dublin) has this passage about Macha:

> *"Macha that is a crow or the three Morrigans that is Macha and Badb and Morrigan, Macha's crop that is the heads of people killed in battle...rough the dwellings there where men shear off Macha's crop where warriors drive a multitude into pens where the raven woman stir up strife."*[16]

While short this text is particularly important as it gives us some valuable insight into Macha as a battle and war goddess.

O'Mulconry's Glossary offers a slightly condensed version of what is found in Irsan, saying:

> *"Macha, that is Badb or one of the three Morrigans, whence Macha's crop that is people's heads after the slaughter."*

O'Clery's Glossary offers this:

> *"Macha, that is a crow or hooded crow, the heap of Macha that is collecting of a crow or a hooded crow."*

This gives us three references to Macha, crows, and battle. The first two refer to severed heads as her nut-crop; the third to what a crow gathers as her "heap" although I believe it's possible this is a later confusion of the earlier saying, given the similarity of the word used for heap with a related word for head. We know that severed heads were highly symbolic and meaningful in Irish culture and can safely assume that the connection between

Macha and these heads is layered and significant, tying her to success in battle.

The *Táin Bó Cúailgne* – Although Macha of the Tuatha De Danann doesn't make an appearance, as such, in the TBC she is referenced at least once when the warrior Fergus meic Roich calls his sword a 'halidom of Macha'; a halidom is a sacred object or something viewed as holy. This ties into Macha as a goddess and again relates her to war and battle.

These sources show us that Macha was strongly associated with her two sisters, Badb and the Morrigan, and reinforces the idea that the three act together as a triad. This pattern is found across Irish myth where groups of three deities, often siblings, are significant together; we might point to the three Brighids as another example of this pattern, or to the three sovereignty goddesses Fotla, Banba, and Eriu.

The material we have to look to also reinforces the idea of Macha as a goddess of war and battle. She stirs up strife and *'bitter fighting'*, the sword is a sacred symbol to her, and the heads of men who die fighting are her *'crop'*. This last ties her directly victory in war as well as to the fighting itself in an inescapable way. This is particularly interesting to consider when we also take into account the Moytura stories which have Macha at the front lines of fighting. Her place as a war goddess then is a set aspect of Macha of the Tuatha De Danann.

Macha's connection to magic is well established across sources, with various texts naming her as a witch, sorceress, and druid. Each of these works a slightly different type of magic, something that we see in Irish myths where we find three distinct main[17] classes of magic workers: tuithecha [witches], corrguinecha [sorcerers], and druad [druids]. In the *Cath Maige Tuired* all three of these groups are called on to contribute their powers to the fight and each responds by promising a different thing: the druids pledge to bring showers of fire on the Fomorians, the sorcerers say they will drain the vigour from the enemy warriors and bind their urine, and the witches promise to enchant the trees, stones, and grass into an army to fight on the side of the Tuatha De. The powers wielded by each of the three have some overlap – in the *Cét-Cath Maige Tuired* it's the sorceresses who rain blood and fire on their enemies, and in a different passage of the *Cath Maige Tuired* the druids drain the vigour from enemies while the sorcerers enchant the earth – but they are generally treated as distinct groups of magical practitioners within the texts. It is perhaps notable that Macha is associated with all three types of magic and is labelled as part of each group in different places, making her a goddess of magic in general and of witches, sorcerers, and druids specifically.

Tuaithe is defined as witchcraft and is related to the word tuath, meaning *"northward, turning northward, perverse, wicked"*. Tuaithe is a complex word that is associated with both the Good Folk (tuath-geinte) as well as witches (tuaithech or bantuaithech), and to make things more complex, although the word tuath has strong negative associations, bantuaithech is also defined as *'wise woman'* and tuaithech by itself only means *"a person with magic powers"*. We might tentatively conclude then that this particular type of witchcraft is associated with the Otherworld and can be sinister in nature or benevolent, rather like the aos sidhe themselves.

Corrguinecht is often translated as sorcery but literally means 'crane-wounding' likely a reference to the crane-pose where the sorcerer would stand on one leg, with one arm behind his back and one eye closed and chant a spell against his enemy, usually in the form of a satire. This kind of magic is seen in the *Cath Maige Tuired* when Lugh uses the crane pose and chant to curse the Fomorians before the battle, and at the start of the *Cét-Cath Maige Tuired* Macha is referred to as a sorceress when she and her two sisters call rains of fire and blood down on the Fir Bolg. Corrguinecht seems particularly suited to use in battle.

Druidecht is the magic of druids; although the term is sometimes translated as wizardry it literally means druid-prowess. Druids in pagan and early Christian Ireland were considered a class of people, skilled in various magic, who acted as advisers to kings. Although most stories of druids feature male characters female druids aren't unheard of. In various translations and versions of the *Táin Bó Cúailgne* Fedelm is called a druidess, seer, or fairy. The Morrigan and Macha are called druidesses at different points and the Tuatha De Danann appeared to have both male and female Druids. In the story of Fionn Mac Cumhaill it is said that he was fostered by two women, one of whom is described as a druidess. A 15th century Irish manuscript relates how Fingin Mac Luchta was visited by a druidess each Samhain eve who would foretell events in the year to come. In all of these cases the word used to describe the woman varied between druidess, seer, and fairy and most were strongly connected to the Otherworld, for example, in the story of Fingin the Druidess was said to come from a fairy hill. It is possible that this reflects the slow Christianization of older stories into more fantastical forms, or the liminal place that druids occupied where they were always seen as being more than one thing, as it were. Female druids were often described as both seers and druids, indicating that perhaps druidesses were often both or were particularly associated with prophecy.

By putting all of these pieces together we can build a more complete picture of who Macha of the Tuatha De Danann was and deepen our understanding of her. Now that we have a better idea of who Macha as an individual is let's look at Macha's family connections, her role among the Tuatha De, and how she fits into or with the Morrigan.

Family Connections

Macha of the Tuatha De Danann is the daughter of Ernmas according to the *Lebor Gabala Erenn*:

> *"Three other daughters moreover had Ernmas, that is Badb and Macha and Morrigu, that is Anand her name."*

These three sisters are often grouped together and form the *'tri Morrignae'* or three Morrigans referenced in sources like *Cormac's Glossary*. Her most significant relationship throughout mythology is definitely with her two sisters. Her father is Delbaeth, who at one point was a king of the Tuatha De Danann, and her mother is Ernmas, described as a farmer. Below we will explore some of her relatives and close connections.

Badb – Another of the three Morrigans, Badb is Macha's sister. Her name means hooded crow but later came to also mean a supernatural woman, witch, or night terror. These three meanings – Badb the goddess, crow, and supernatural woman/ witch – can cause a lot of confusion in a story if the context isn't entirely clear. Badb is particularly associated with the slaughter and cranage of war and with prophecy.

Morrigan – The Morrigan is the most prominent of the three sisters and the one that appears in most stories. Her name may be understood as either 'great queen' or 'queen of phantoms' and she is a driving force in most of the stories she appears in. Although not referred to by her personal name, only by title, the Morrigan is clearly a distinct individual in stories, often acting alone and sometimes acting with her two sisters. Macalister on his notes in the *Lebor Gabala Erenn* suggests that the Morrigan and Badb originally acted as paired deities and that Macha was added in later, but whether or not that's the case they are strongly linked with each other now. The Morrigan is a complex goddess who is associated with war, battle, prophecy, incitement, satire, sovereignty, magic, and victory.

Ernmas – One of, if not the, most prolific of the Tuatha de Danann, Ernmas had at least 12 children including Macha. Of her five sons and seven daughters, the trio of Morrigan sisters and the trio of sovereignty goddesses (Banba, Fotla, and Eriu) are the most well-known and often discussed. Ernmas's name means 'iron death' in older Irish and although she is named as a farmer in the *Lebor Gabala Erenn* she falls in battle against the Fir Bolg suggesting that she was a warrior which would make sense with her name.

Delbaeth – There are multiple beings named Delbaeth in Irish mythology; the one who seems to be Macha's father was a king of the Tuatha De Danann at one point and is the son of Ogma. Listed as her father in some versions of the Lebor Gabala Erenn, he is also the father of many of her siblings. The meaning of his name is uncertain, but the *Dindshenchas* break the name down to 'dolb aed' or roughly 'magical fire'.

Midhir – Alternately, the *Dindshenchas* names Midhir as Macha's father; although this is a reference to a different Macha, Macha the Fairy woman (who will be discussed in the next chapter) I did want to mention this here as both are members of the Tuatha De Danann. Midhir is one of the Dagda's sons and possesses the sidhe of Brí Leith in Ardagh.

Deala mac Loich – A final option for her father is mentioned by Elizabeth Grey in her notes on the *Cath Maige Tuired*. He is an obscure figure that we don't know much about. The first part of his name is uncertain, deala may be related to a word for greediness or for affection or even for the proper order, each of which would give a very different tone to the character. 'Mac Loich' is easier and means Son of a Warrior.

Banba, Fotla, and Ériu – Macha's three other sisters (who also, like her, appear within a grouping of three) are the main sovereignty goddesses of Ireland. According to the *Lebor Gabala Erenn* the Gaels [read: humans] only attained possession of Ireland because these three goddesses granted it to them in exchange for the island bearing their names. Fotla and Banba are now considered archaic terms for Ireland, but Ériu is the root of the modern name Eire. According to Foras Feasa Ar Erenn these three worshipped the three Morrigan sisters, although Keating offers no explanation as to why.

Nuada – Nuada was the king of the Tuatha De Danann when they first arrived in Ireland. In the battle against the Fir Bolg, he lost his arm, which was replaced with one of silver,[18] and because of this injury could no longer be king. Seven years later the original arm was restored allowing him to return to kingship and he stepped up to overthrow the king who had followed him, Bres, because of his poor rulership. According to the *Cath Maige Tuired* he died in the fight with the Fomorians, alongside Macha. Although she is never named as his wife in any story it is widely assumed to be true, and has become a common modern piece of folklore. At the least we can say that they fought and died together at the battle of Maige Tuired.

Macha of the Tuatha De Danann is a complex figure, more so perhaps than the other versions we've already discussed because we have more information about her. We know that she arrived with the Tuatha De Danann when they first came to Ireland and that she acted with her sisters during this time to magically attack the Fir Bolg and to go to the battle field with the warriors. There is no question that Macha is a member of the Tuatha De and that she acts in alignment with that, fighting in the battle against the Fomorians and falling with Nuada there (although we should keep in mind the transient nature of death with the Irish gods). This gives us a good amount of evidence that Macha was a warrior herself and would fight in the battle directly. Whereas the earlier iterations of Macha we discussed in Chapter 1 and 2 had connections to creation and civilization, Macha of the Tuatha De Danann is linked to the opposite energy, to that of battle and death.

Macha as Morrigan is a more difficult topic, because there are some strongly divergent views on the subject. For some modern pagans Macha is understood as one facet or face of the Morrigan, one piece within a whole; in this understanding she exists within the Morrigan, who is an individual being that can manifest three different identities or personalities. In older sources she is never described this way but always mentioned in the context of an individual who is one of three distinct beings given the title of Morrigan. In this view the sisters act as a cohesive group but exist separately from each other as unique individuals. The three-in-one view is fairly widespread now, and the one-of-three view is less widely discussed.

Macha's connections to her two sisters are a significant aspect of who Macha of the Tuatha De is, and I don't think we can easily separate out her as a part of this triad and her as one of the Tuatha De Danann, because both identities are linked to each other; in almost all the references we have to her in mythology she is mentioned with the Morrigan and Badb, with the three presenting as a unit. In any case Macha is widely understood in this material as a deity of war and battle.

Macha in My Life – the Mound of Hostages

The main way Macha tends to be understood today is as one of the three Morrigans, as one part of a greater whole, but I have always found her to be a powerful goddess in her own right, and one who can appear with the Morrigan without being eclipsed by her. I experienced this for myself once in 2016, when I was visiting Teamhair [Tara] with a group. We wandered around the site, taking our time so we could experience as much of the amazing landscape as possible. I recited the Morrigan's peace prophecy for the group near the Lia Fal and at one point I went to Dumha na nGiall [mound of hostages] the place in the *Cét-Cath Maige Tuired* where the Morrigan, Badb, and Macha had stood to curse the Fir Bolg. Standing there I had a visionary experience of all three of the Morrigans on the grassy dome of the mound, each distinct but clearly working together. Badb was on the left, clad in a cloak of black feathers, looking down and murmuring; the Morrigan stood in the middle, a fierce looking red-haired woman in leather armour, looking up with her arms raised, singing; Macha was on the right in a red tunic,[19] arms stretched out towards the horizon, chanting. They were each very different and doing slightly different things, but at the same time they were united and somehow it all flowed smoothly together. I didn't feel like Macha was eclipsed by the Morrigan or there in a supportive role, but rather that the three were on equal footing and working together.

It was one of many intense experiences I had on that trip, and one that stands out even today. It helped me see the three Morrigans in a new way, as deities who worked closely together but not as interchangeable names for one being. It also helped me to appreciate Macha, even within this triad, for herself and to see her magic and power not as part of the Morrigans but as complimentary to it.

Chapter 4

Macha of the Sidhe

"My name," said she, "and the name of that which I shall bear, will forever cleave to the place of this assembly. I am Macha, daughter of Sainreth mac Imbaith."

–The Debility of the Ulstermen

The Story – the Noinden Ulaid[20]

Once there was a wealthy farmer in Ard Macha [Armagh] named Crunnchu, son of Agnoman, who had four sons with his wife before she died, leaving him a widower. One day he was alone in his house when a beautiful, well-dressed young woman came in. She spoke to no one but tended the fire, cooked the afternoon meal, and milked the cow. When she came back in, she turned around to the right then went into the kitchen and began instructing the servants, before going to sit next to Crunnchu at the table. After the meal she sat up until everyone had gone to bed, then banked the fire before turning around to the right a second time and then joined Crunnchu in his bed where they lay together. She found him very attractive and with her as his wife his wealth grew even greater.

Then the day came for Ulster's assembly[21] and Crunnchu said that he would like to go. Macha advised him not to, saying that their marriage would continue only if he never spoke of her at the assembly. He swore he wouldn't do so, and so he left to go to the gathering with the rest of the local people. Once there he saw all manner of contests and entertainment, and well into the long day the king's chariot horses were brought out to race; they were the finest pair of horses seen in Ireland and all the people praised their beauty and speed. Hearing this Crunnchu couldn't stop himself from saying that his wife could run even faster than these animals.

King Conchobar overheard this and angrily ordered Crunnchu to be seized by his soldiers and held until Macha could be brought to show the truth of the matter. The king sent messengers to Macha, to bring Macha back and she welcomed them when they arrived, asking why they had come, only to be informed that she had to go to the assembly to free him. She protested that she was in labour and about to give birth and couldn't go, but agreed after the messengers told her Crunnchu would be executed otherwise.

When she arrived at the assembly the people crowded around, despite her pleas that it was shameful for her to be seen so heavily pregnant[22] and labouring. She asked why she had been brought and the crowd yelled that it was to race the horses, to which she replied that she was soon to deliver her child – but hearing this Conchobar ordered Crunnchu to be killed. She begged the crowd to show her mercy, reminding them that each had been born of a mother and asking for only a small delay to give birth.[23]. The king refused and order her to race, and hearing that she told them that their treatment of her was unacceptable and that they would be infamous for it. The king asked her name then and she told him she was Macha, daughter of Sainreth son of Imbaith, and that her name would forever be on that place. The race began and she ran faster than the wind, passing the horses easily and crossing the finish line well before them. She fell to her knees then and cried out, giving birth to a son and a daughter before the horses passed her.

Everyone who heard her cry out was seized with the same weakness of a woman in childbirth, and she proclaimed that because of their hard heartedness the whole province of Ulster would be afflicted the same way for five days and four nights[24] whenever they were in the greatest need, with only women, children, and Cu Chulainn[25] exempt from the curse. After pronouncing this fate on the assembly Macha and her children disappeared into the Otherworld.[26]

Because of the twins she bore there the place was named Emhain[27] Macha, a name it still bears today.

This is the story that we have for Macha of the Sidhe sometimes called Macha the Fairy Woman, and unlike Macha of the Tuatha De Danann she appears only in this single myth. Despite that there is a good amount of information provided in the story and a lot to discuss about this figure. We will look at the family associated with this Macha and then dive into some context for Irish fairy beliefs and how Macha fits into that.

Family Relationships

Macha as daughter of Midhir – This is a claim we find in the Edinburgh Dindshenchas, which calls Macha *'the sun of womanhood'* and daughter of Midhir. Midhir is one of the Tuatha De Danann, a son of the Dagda, and king of the sidhe of Brí Leith in Ardagh.

Macha as daughter of Sainreth – Sainreth is an obscure figure whose name may translate to 'a particular characteristic' or defining quality in a person.

Fír – Macha's son according to the Dindshenchas, his name means 'truth'.

Fíal – Macha's daughter, twin sister to Fír, her name means 'honour' or 'modesty'

Crunnchu – His name appears in a few variants across the stories; the meaning is uncertain. He is described as a wealthy farmer, a man who wouldn't have been nobility but would still have held a high social standing. We know from the story that he was a widower and had at least four children prior to Macha's arrival.

Fairies in Irish Myth & Folklore

This is, of course, a massive topic that entire books can be written about, so here we will only be focusing on a few highlights. I have a book, *Pagan Portals – Aos Sidhe,* for those who would like a deeper dive into these beliefs.

Macha appears in this story as a woman of the Sidhe, coming into the human world for her own obscure purpose and choosing to become the wife of a mortal man. It is important here then to give some context to beliefs around the sidhe [otherworldly hills] in Ireland which are different from ideas about fairies in popculture. The Irish Aos Sidhe [people of the otherworldly hills] often appear very similar to humans, but with an Otherworldly aura to them; they are sometimes said to be extremely beautiful but in other stories may be described as looking just like any of the local human population. They are said to live in the sidhe and can travel between the human world and Otherworld freely. In various stories they may also live on mythic islands found in the sea and, in some others, they are associated with particular trees. In all cases they are seen as beings who are adjacent to but distinct from humanity, in the same way their world is.

The Aos Sidhe are powerful beings who can influence humans in various ways, from effecting their luck to health, for good or ill. They can do this directly via elfshot, an invisible fairy arrow which can make a person or animal sick, and the fairy-touch which can drive a person mad, or they can use their magic. In most stories the Aos Sidhe only cause harm in response to some offense – although what they consider offensive isn't what a human might – but in some cases they don't seem to need any motivation. They are known to occasionally steal humans, from infants to young people, to new brides and new mothers, to add to their own population or to serve them in some fashion. The Aos sidhe also possess a kind of magic that distorts human sense and can cause a human to perceive the world around them in whatever way the aos sidhe want. They are respected and feared, and many protections exist to prevent their interference in human life.

It is also established across folk belief that both the Tuatha De Danann and the Aos Sidhe can and may reproduce with humans. Various families trace their lineage back to members of the Tuatha De and some families share stories of ancestors among the sidhe-folk. This is an important thing to understand when listening to or reading the story of Macha of the sidhe, who takes a mortal husband and bears him children, because those aspects of the tale are not unique to Macha.

Macha as a Fairy Bride

Macha here fits the description of a fairy bride, a woman of the sidhe who marries a mortal (Clark, 1991). Fairy brides always bring blessings with them and also a prohibition that cannot be broken or the marriage will immediately end. In this case that prohibition is that Crunnchu must not speak of her to the people of the assembly, or perhaps to anyone outside the household. When he breaks his promise not to do so Macha must leave him, although luckily for him she chooses to go to race first, thus saving his life. In most tales like this the fairy wife or lover leaves immediately and the human spouse is unable to stop them going. The only other tale I am aware of where a fairy bride acts to save her lover even after he betrays his promise is found in the Arthurian tale of Sir Lanaval, where – like Crunnchu – Lanaval has been put under a prohibition not to speak of his fairy mistress but does so anyway; he is told to either produce this fairy woman to prove his story or die and moved by some love or pity for him the fairy woman chooses to come and save his life. In the same way Macha is given the option to simply leave but chooses instead to go to the assembly to save her mortal husband.

Generally, when a fairy bride leaves, she also takes with her both the luck she brought as well as any property; she may or may not take her half-human children with her. Briggs describes fairy brides as both tragic and wonderful, as they emphasize the enchantment of the fairy world and its inhabitants but also always end in tragedy for the human (Briggs, 1976). In Macha's case she doesn't take anything away with her except her children, although there are versions of the story where only she leaves or is said to die, however, even in the versions where she lives one can easily argue that her curse on the men of Ulster, while justified, counts as a tragic ending of the story.

Macha of the Sidhe is a unique figure, one who isn't connected to either colonization/cultivating a new place or warfare but to the domestic sphere, despite being the quintessential outsider. However, in this story as in the earlier iterations of Macha she is strongly connected to magic, in this case specifically cursing. Her curse echoes the battle magic of Macha of the Tuatha De, by impacting the Ulstermen when they are in a time of great need and physically weakening them. Here we see Macha as a force of justice, where her curse isn't given from maliciousness but from righteous anger at being greatly wronged. She is humiliated in front of the crowd and forced to give birth in the dirt of the race track, and her curse enacts justice by making those who caused her pain feel for themselves what it is to give birth, to be weak, to be helpless when facing difficulties. The names of her two children – truth and honour – reflect this as well by showing that she is in the right, following a pattern in Irish myth where children born in a story often have names reflecting their circumstances or nature. This Macha is a strong figure who embodies perseverance and determination against great odds which ties in to her other iterations as well.

Macha of the fairies could very easily be the same figure as Macha of the Tuatha De Danann, because when humans arrived in Ireland all of the Tuatha De went into the sidhe and became Aos Sidhe, joining the population that was already there. Macha of the Tuatha De is said to have died in the *Cath Maige Tuired*, but death is ephemeral and impermanent for the Irish gods, so it isn't a stretch in my opinion to see her as eternal and as one of the Aos Sidhe in the same way all the other Tuatha De Danann are. It is true she is given different parentage in these myths, but the genealogy of the gods is convoluted and often contradictory so I'm not sure that alone is enough to differentiate these figures. In the story Macha is called a 'banscál', a complicated term which can mean a warrior woman or woman in general, but the term scál has older connotations of a supernatural figure or phantom. So banscál could also mean supernatural woman, further connecting her to the sidhe but also perhaps to the gods within the Otherworldly mounds. It is food for thought at least.

Macha in My Life – Emhain Macha

I was able to visit Emhain Macha – also known as Navan Fort – in 2016 when I was in Armagh with a group tour. Emhain Macha historically was the site of the seat of power of Ulster, from which kings ruled and it shows continues occupation since the neolithic. The location includes several important sites: two mounds, one of which is believed to have been a main ceremonial site; what is said in local folklore to be the racetrack from the story; a stone that folklore claims is where Macha gave birth; and a modern recreation of a small Iron Age settlement.[28]

I visited on the first of November, Samhain,[29] and went first to the Iron Age settlement area. It was fun to hear the re-enactors telling stories and to experience what life in that time may have been like. After this we walked towards the mound itself and on the way, we passed the place that is, according to local belief, the location of the racetrack where Macha ran and near that a stone that (also according to local folklore) marks the place where Macha gave birth. I paused here for several minutes, just looking at everything and thinking of how strongly Macha's story is embedded in that land. It was very moving to stand where tales say Macha herself stood, to stand where she raced, and birthed, and left the human world. Although I don't believe the myths are literally true there was still a numinous feeling there, enmeshed with the trees, and stones, and earth by the countless generations who had been there and talked of Macha, who believed that she had stood there, run there. It is impossible to properly put the feeling into words.

Eventually we moved on to the main mound at the site, the location of the original fort. It is a small, steep hill surrounded by trees, somewhat challenging to climb but worth the effort. Standing at the summit I found myself drawn to a smaller site just to the side of the main one, and I went over there to connect to the place. It was a moving experience but the feelings at the stone were more intense. There was something about standing there imagining the race and the curse that moved me more deeply than visiting the main archaeological site nearby.

With the Irish gods I believe it is important to try to visit the places that anchor their stories, to see and experience for one's self what it is to stand where these beings are once said to have stood. I know that isn't possible for everyone, for a variety of reasons, and if you can't have this opportunity, I think that utilizing online virtual tours or pictures may also work. Too often, especially as Americans, people may not grasp how entrenched Irish myth is in the landscape, the way that story and place intertwine, and I think that understanding is vital. The Gods and spirits can and do go where they please but nonetheless appreciating the earth and stone and tress that anchor their stories in this world is vital. It makes the gods immediate and present in ways that simply hearing the stories doesn't.

Chapter 5

Macha of the Red Hair

"This Aedh left no children but one daughter, Macha Mong-Ruadh [that is, Redhaired Macha] was her name. She demanded her father's turn of the sovereignty. Cimbaeth and Dithorba said that they would not give sovereignty to a woman."

– O'Curry, 1861

The Story[30]

Once long ago[31] Ireland was ruled by three kings, Dithorba, Aedh Rua,[32] and Cimbaeth, who took turns sharing the kingship, with each ruling for seven years. This agreement had been reached with a great many sureties offered by each man, effectively hostages and treasure that would be forfeited is they failed to hold up their portion of the agreement. They went through this process three full times with each ruling three times for seven years until 63 years passed, and then Aedh drowned leaving only one child, Macha Mongruadh [Macha of the Red Hair]. When her father's time to rule came again she demanded her father's share of the sovereignty of Ireland but Dithorba and Cimbaeth said they wouldn't let a woman rule.

Macha fought against the other two for rulership of Ireland and won, taking her place as queen. She ruled for seven years, during which Dithorba died leaving behind five sons: Baeth [fool], Bras [boastful], Betach [shameless], Uallach [arrogant], and Borbchas [rudeness]. When seven years had passed Cimbaeth and Dithorba's sons expected her to step aside for them but she refused, saying that her reign wasn't from an agreement, as her father's had been, but from might of arms because she had won the crown through battle. When they tried to fight her she won again, driving the five sons into exile and finally taking Cimbaeth as her husband and giving him the responsibility of her soldiers.

The five sons fled into the wilderness and took to raiding and pillaging those around them, but no one was able to apprehend them. Macha left the kingdom in Cimbaeth's hands and went to capture them and stop the trouble they were causing in the land. She took rye dough and rubbed it over herself, dressed in rags, and went in this disguise to Connacht to find the brothers. She came across them camping for the night, sitting around a fire, and told them she was a poor old woman cast out into the wilderness. They offered her food and then demanded that she sleep with each of them in payment for it. The eldest went with her into the woods where she quickly subdued and bound him before returning to the fire. The other brothers thought that the eldest hadn't returned because he must be embarrassed about going with her and so they each go alone in turn and she ties them all up. Thus, captured she leads them back to her royal palace where the people all demand the brothers be killed for their crimes. Macha, however, refuses to do this, saying that instead they will be held as prisoners until they build her a fort, and uses her brooch pin to outline the place she wants the boundary trench dug for this. In this way their lives were spared and Macha's fort was built. And so Emhain Macha is named from Eómain meaning a neck-brooch, hence Macha's Brooch.[33]

Gearóid Ó Crualaoich offers a metaphysical interpretation of Macha Mongruadh in *The Book of the Cailleach,* highlighting the meaning of her father's name – Aedh the Red – her epithet of Mongruadh [red haired] and the place of her father's death, a waterfall named Ess Ruad [red waterfall] and pointing out the connection between the colour red[34] and the Otherworld. This implies that Macha Mongruadh, like Macha of the sidhe, had an Otherworldly origin. Similarly, the site of her father's death is the place where the salmon of knowledge[35] lived, connecting Aedh to both the Otherworld and great wisdom. Ó Crualaoich suggests that Macha represented divine and Otherworldly sovereignty and that her taking the crown after her father's death was symbolic of the divine feminine controlling sovereignty across Irish stories. This is based on a wider pattern across Irish belief that it was a goddess who granted a king the right to rule, often depicted by his marriage to that goddess or to the land itself. Rosalind Clark shares this approach, describing Macha Mongraudh as an euhemerized goddess whose magical abilities have been converted in the tale to martial prowess.

This Macha is positioned in her story as a historical or pseudo-historical queen, a woman who ruled at a time when that was very uncommon. Pseudohistorical material is that which is framed as real history but which is likely to be myth instead, so that the mythic story is set in a very grounded real-world way. This approach grounds a story in the history of a place or people without being overtly magical or mythic in nature and presents the characters of the story as extraordinary humans. It is not uncommon to find deities appearing as humans in pseudohistory, usually through the process of euhemerization where an otherwise supernatural or divine character is explained as a human who has previously been misunderstood as supernatural. We see this with other stories of the Tuatha De Danann where they are explained away as humans from Scythia or similar.[36] In this case Macha's framing as a human queen shouldn't be taken to mean that she wasn't a goddess, at least originally, nor that the gods of Ireland were humans that later came to be thought of as gods – in fact the exact opposite is the case with euhemerization.

Although Macha of the red hair may seem like the least likely candidate of the various Machas for being understood as an aspect of the goddess scholars generally agree she is a connected to the others. As Mark Williams points out in his book *Ireland's Immortals* the idea of a deity being re-formed into a literary or mythic character that seems to contradict or differ from the original deity isn't uncommon in Irish mythology. One hint of Macha's divine nature may be found in an account of the naming of Emain Macha in Cormac's Glossary, where Mach is aid to have drawn the boundary of her fort with her neck brooch while sitting down, a feat that would be impossible unless she was truly gigantic (Clark, 1991). Beyond that and the above discussed interpretations of the colour red in her story the idea is also supported through her eponymous connections to Ard Macha and Emhain Macha, illustrated here:

> *"Macha Red-mane, daughter of Aed, was nurse of Ugane of the combats, and wife of urbane Cimbaith son of Fintan: until death he never avoided a fight. It was for Emain and Ard Macha her perilous battles were fought, a rough exploit. She ruled uprightly for seven years"*
>
> – Banshenchus

These connections to place are shared by Macha of the Sidhe and Macha of the Nemedians, and indicate Macha's role as a sovereignty goddess and as a creator deity, a being who both shaped the land and who gives sovereignty over it. That last can be seen with Macha of the Red Hair because she was a queen who ruled after earning the title in combat and who chose the roles the other kings would have. The overturning of social norms and expectations would be strange for humans of the time but perfectly align with ideas about the divine Otherworldly woman judging the worthiness of potential kings and controlling who would come to the throne (Ó Crualaoich, 2003). As an Irish Goddess of sovereignty Macha is a conveyor of flaithius,[37] who grants the right to rule to the one most fit to do so. It is she who can appear from the Otherworld bringing either good or bad luck to the people as she chooses (Clark, 1991). We see this exemplified in the story of Macha Mongruadh who refuses to submit to her father's co-kings, becomes queen by her own hand and only then marries one of the other kings who is clearly subservient in position to her.

Sovereignty is a complex topic today, and one that is often interpreted in two very different, even opposing ways. Historically and by the dictionary, sovereignty is supreme power of a government to rule itself and those within its control, while in modern contexts sovereignty is often used interchangeably with autonomy, the right of an individual to lead their own life. When we talk about Macha as a sovereignty goddess we are generally speaking of her power to grant or withhold a throne from a potential monarch, and to control the welfare, prosperity and luck of those within her domain (in this case Armagh). However, many people today also see her as a goddess of personal sovereignty (i.e. autonomy) who helps individuals find the strength to enforce their own will and control their own life.

Neither of these views is wrong, and although they seem to be contradictory in nature they reflect the layered understanding we need around Macha and sovereignty. In her older stories she is a power behind the throne, or as with Macha Mongruadh sitting on it, and as such is supporting a monarchy and its related government. She is a goddess who looks to the wider view of what is best for an entire group or kingdom and then acts to either support the king who is nurturing that view or acts to undermine and take down a king that isn't ruling well. In a modern context she is a force that supports people, especially women, who are seeking strength and control within their lives, and she is often called on or looked to by people who feel like they aren't in control for her aid in returning that sense of personal sovereignty. An example of this in the 21st century can be seen with the House of Apples program Macha's Justice, which offers support to survivors of domestic abuse.

While sovereignty is an important aspect of Macha of the Red Hair, it isn't the only thing that she is associated with; war and battle are also key aspects to this Macha, as they were with Macha of the Tuatha De Danann. She leads an army and wins, as well as later pursuing her enemies personally, displaying her ability on the battlefield as well as her leadership (Ó Crualaoich, 2003). Although she defeats the five sons of the rival king through cunning rather than violence, her willingness to seek them out alone and capture them shows her mettle as a warrior.

Macha of the Red Hair is a powerful figure: as a human character she inspires women to fight for their rights and their autonomy; as a goddess she shapes the land and creates order within chaos, as well as granting rulership to the rightful king. She is a humanized version of the divine Macha, a relatable face of the Great Queen, and the fifth and final aspect of Macha found across Irish mythology. Understanding her in this story helps us better understand Macha in general, the figure who exists within each of these aspects and together forms a whole divine being, because only by looking at the entirety of Macha can we hope to grasp the wider symbolism and power of this goddess.

Macha in My Life – Another Kind of Healing

My main deity of the three Morrigans, the one I formally dedicated to in the mid 2000's, is Macha. I find Her to be very much a Goddess of women's rights and empowerment, themes which came up often during that period of dedication. In following Them, and Her, I have been led on many interesting adventures and met some wonderful people. They are not easy Goddesses though, although perhaps none of the Gods are, and the saying that you will sometimes hear that *'with the Morrigan there is always a cost'* I believe is true. I have been very blessed by

Them, but I have also paid for that blessing both in the things I have done for Them and in the standards that I know I am held to. There is something relentless in Them that I admire and it pushes me to do my best for Them.

I first began connecting to Macha, and the three Morrigans more generally, in 1999 when I had received a message during a group meditation/Journey where They, collectively, told me that what I was meant to do for Them was to be a healer. I was surprised and disappointed, to be honest. I'd always fancied myself quite the diviner and I'd spent many years learning a variety of divination methods to a point that I thought I was very good with them. I took pride in my skill, and while I had some small interest in healing it wasn't anything I could picture myself really focusing on.

It's dangerous to assume things. You see when I was told I needed to focus on healing I assumed that meant physical, practical healing. Like fix a broken arm healing or the more New Age re-balance someone's energy healing. And that was just about the last thing I wanted to dedicate my life to doing, even in service to a trio of Goddesses. I wasn't even questioning why that particular grouping would want me, of all people, to be a healer – I was too busy making faces and groaning. In my defence I was 20 at the time, headstrong, and prone to melodramatic reactions.

I did start learning a wide array of healing methods though and started studying magical healing work from a traditional witchcraft perspective. I even briefly looked into massage therapy school before deciding it wasn't a good fit for me. I started trying to do more magical healing, at least, and it wasn't like it was horrible but it definitely wasn't making my soul do cart wheels of satisfaction either. I felt frustrated, more than anything, but I was trying to trust that, ultimately, They were taking me where I needed to be.

But during this period an interesting thing was happening. Although very few people at that time knew I honoured the Morrigans, I started running into Her followers on a very regular basis, even in the most unexpected of places. And the conversations often turned to ways these people had been hurt by life or other people, ways they'd been abused, ways they felt devalued, ways they were questioning their worth. And over and over I'd end up sharing my own story, my own struggle to recover a sense of sovereignty and self after victimization and over and over they'd tell me that I'd helped them feel more whole, more empowered. I found myself opening up to strangers about my own past, my own pain, and becoming an advocate for the beauty of brokenness and the potential to heal even when we have lost all sense of personal value. I found myself speaking out against the very idea of being ashamed for being a victim, and speaking instead about the power of the survivor. The strength of knowing exactly what you can endure. Then this started to happen more generally, a push to help people see their own power, their own value, their own worth, even when they had been broken. Especially when they had been broken.

And finally – not quickly – finally I realized that healing is a layered word, and that what They wanted from me, what They'd always wanted from me, wasn't to physically heal people or magically heal people but to heal people's sense of sovereignty. Sometimes this is through encouraging words, and sometimes this is through a challenge, because They can be hard even in healing, but the result is growth and strength. Even 26 years later I'm not sure I do this well, but at least now I know what I'm supposed to be doing, and now it feels right and I enjoy doing it. I joke now that She sends people to me when She needs to, but it's only partially a joke; when my service is needed the person will find me.

Chapter 6

Putting It All Together

"Rough the dwelling places there
Where men shear off Macha's crop
Where warriors drive a multitude into pens
Where the raven women stir up strife."
– Sanas Cormaic (translation by me)

Thus far we have looked at the different appearances of Macha across the mythology, exploring each individual story, the themes connected to them, and the ways each might – or might not – intertwine with the others. Now we will move into looking at Macha as a cohesive being by discussing the particular things that she is most associated with or connected to. This will include both historic ideas as well as some modern ones that people embrace today.

This chapter is going to be wide ranging and will be broken down into smaller subsections for each category. The goal is to cover all the major points in ways that will help people both better understand Macha and the various things that she is connected to or associated with.

Colours – From a strictly historic perspective we have no knowledge of colours associated with Macha by Irish pagans, however, modern pagans have developed some based on hints in stories. *The Banshenchus* refer to Macha as 'the sun of womanhood' and some people associate her with red because of that, while others connect red to her because of Macha Mongruadh's red hair. Black is associated with all three of the Morrigan sisters because of their strong association with black birds, particularly crows and ravens. She may also be associated with the colour grey because in the *Ulster Cycle* Cu Chulainn has a horse from the Otherworld named the grey of Macha.

Symbols – As with colours there is no clear idea of what pre-Christian Irish people would have considered a symbol of Macha, if they even had any. In modern paganism some people associate the triskele or triquetra with the Morrigan more generally. People may also wear pendants with horses or crows for Macha specifically.

Associations – Macha has a range of associations that apply to either all or most of her aspects. These include sovereignty, magic, witchcraft and Druidry, war, battle, death, and prophecy. Her connection to sovereignty has been discussed in several previous chapters. Her connection to magic can be seen in Macha of the Tuatha De as well as Macha of the sidhe, both of whom use magic to achieve their ends, one through battle magic that defends her community and the other through a curse to punish those who have wronged her. Related to this Macha of the Tuatha De is explicitly called both a witch and druid in the source material (as are all three Morrigan collectively). Macha of the Tuatha De and Macha of the Redhair are both strongly connected to war and battle, and by extension death, so that she may represent the side of the fertile land Goddess that is sovereignty personified as war (Waddell, 2014). And we see prophecy coming in with Macha of the Nemedians who predicted the *Táin Bó Cúailgne* before dying of a broken heart.

Ulster – Macha is strongly tied to Ulster in Northern Ireland. Her name is used in some myths as a synonym for Ulster itself or for Armagh specifically, as we see in the *Silva Gadelica* where saint Patrick says *"he shall go to serve Macha in the north..."* referencing the location not the pagan goddess (O'Grady, 1892). In a range of sources from that time Macha was used to refer to either Ard Macha or Emain Macha and the surrounding areas. This connection between Macha and Ulster would particularly hold true for three aspects of Macha; Macha wife of Nemed, Macha of the Sidhe, and Macha Mongruadh who gave their names to geography in Ulster further associating them with the land there.

Ard Macha – 'Macha's height', Anglicized as Armagh the name belongs to both a city and county in Northern Ireland. *The Dindshenchas* connect both Macha of the Nemedians and Macha of the Sidhe to Ard Macha, which is named for them in different stories.

Emhain Macha – The main location associated with Macha's is Emhain Macha (Navan Fort) located in Navan, county Armagh, Northern Ireland. This site was once the seat of power in the area, one of the three biggest ritual sites in Ireland, and was in use from the neolithic period forward. Evidence suggests that during the Bronze age, approximately 800 BCE, a timber structure existed at the site of the main mound which was replaced by another similar structure in the Iron age, around 400 BCE (Halpin & Newman, 2006). This was then rebuilt again in the 1st century BCE, then filled with stones – possibly from a previous neolithic cairn – before being burnt[38] and covered over with dirt creating the mound as it is today (Halpin & Newman, 2006; Lynn, 2003). The reason this was done is uncertain with some scholars suggesting it was meant to be a ritual offering of the space to the Otherworld, while others suggest that it was done to contain or focus the Otherworld's influence within that space or create a sidhe, or Otherworldly hall, there (Lynn, 2003; Warner, 2000; Waddell, 2014). Today Navan Fort and Centre maintains the site, including the mound, and has a visitor centre and reconstructed Iron Age village featuring reenactors portraying life at that time.

Emain Macha was a flourishing ritual site for centuries and archaeology can offer valuable insight into Macha and this location by telling us what animals were sacrificed there. Macha is strongly associated with horses, discussed in depth below, and although horse sacrifice was not a main focus in Ireland archaeology has shown that unlike other bronze and Iron Age ritual sites like Dún Ailinne and Teamhair, both located in central Ireland, horses were only extremely rarely sacrificed at Emhain Macha – making up less than only 0.8% of all faunal deposits compared to 5.5% at Teamhair and 2.4% at Dun Ailinne (McCormick, 2009). It's also interesting to note that although cattle were the main deposits at both of the other sites by significant amounts, it was pigs that were the main animal offered at Emain Macha (McCormick, 2009).

Oenach[39] Macha – Macha's role as a Goddess of sovereignty is seen in several key ways, one of the clearest being her association with the oenacha, or Lughnasa fairs, which occurred in August, usually across several weeks. The word oenach is explained in *Cormac's Glossary* as meaning horse races, and the fairs themselves were well known for horse racing (Patterson, 1994). Emhain Macha has a long tradition of these fairs and it is said in the *Prose Dindshenchas* that the Oenach Macha was established in remembrance of Macha of the Red Hair (Waddell, 2014). This yearly harvest fair celebration was not only named for the eponymous Goddess of Emhain Macha but also prominently featured horses being raced. Waddell theorizes that the strong connection to horses at Oenach Macha may reflect both Macha's role as a horse Goddess and also possible earlier ceremonies at the site which would have connected the king to the Goddess ritually (Waddell, 2014). Interestingly another, possibly older, name for Lughnasa is Brón Trogain – *"sorrow of earth"* – which may be as MacNeill suggests in her book *The Festival of Lughnasa*: *"a metaphor for birth"* (MacNeill, 1962, page 10). This could suggest a connection, at least tenuously, between Macha of the Sidhe and the horse race she ran at an oenach with the horse races and celebration of Lughnasa. Each of the Irish Goddesses associated with Lughnasa celebrations including Macha, Tailtiu, and Carman is also a deity who was known for her motherhood, for dying in childbirth, or for dying after clearing plains (Sjoestedt, 2000).

Ravens – A less substantial connection than crows, Macha is nonetheless associated with ravens. The *Sanas Cormaic* calls her and her sisters, Badb and the Morrigan, *'raven women'*, and as discussed above the holiday of Lughnasa was once known by the name Brón Trogain, with the term trogain having meanings that included female ravens specifically.

One of the most well-known birds of omen is the raven. Anytime ravens are in the area their activity, calls and direction of flight might be noted and interpreted, as they are generally seen as an ill omen. If a raven arrives just as a new task is being begun it is seen as an omen that the work will not end well, and a raven near a home signifies a death (O hOgain, 1995). A raven hovering over a herd of livestock was thought to indicate disease among the stock, and to steal a raven's egg would result in the death of a human child (Anderson, 2008).

Crows – Although both Badb and the Morrigan are more strongly connected to crows than Macha, she does still have some connection to them. In some versions of the *Aided Conchulann* all three sisters appear as crows and circle over the place where Cu Chulainn is dying, showing that she could and did take on this form. Additionally in older Irish the word, Macha could refer to either a milking yard/field or a hooded crow. The hooded crow or Royston crow (corvus cornix) is a bird found across Ireland; the name hooded crow is an allusion to the bird's colouring, grey with a black head, wings, and tail, which gives the impression the crow is wearing a hood. The connection of her name to this bird reinforces Macha's wider connection to them, as illustrated in this excerpt from *O'Clery's Glossary*: "Macha .i. badhb no feannóg" Macha that is a hooded crow or Royston crow, where all three terms represent synonyms for the same crow.

Crows are seen as a mix of good and bad omens. It was believed that witches, fairies, mná sidhe [banshees], and Badb appeared as hooded crows in Ireland, a belief that was especially strong in county Clare, and were thus seen as unlucky (Anderson, 2008). As with ravens a crow landing on the roof of a house or flying over a home was an omen of death or disaster, but others believe that bad luck comes when crows leave an area (O hOgain, 1995; Anderson, 2008).

Horses – That Macha is a horse Goddess is often simply assumed and many sources state it as a fact including Waddell and Clark. Macha is often compared to other horse goddesses, including Rhiannon and Epona; even though the meaning of their names varies greatly and their stories are not cohesive they are treated as equivalents across cultures (Waddell, 2014). It is likely that her association with horses is drawn from both her connection to Cu Chulainn's horse, Liath Macha, and the myth where she races against the king's horses, and Waddell further suggests that the horse races held at her main ritual site on Lughnasa may also contribute to this connection. It may further be assumed from the way horses were only rarely sacrificed at Emhain Macha, as it was a common early Irish belief that one shouldn't kill or eat an animal strongly connected to the person; this is shown in the prohibition against charioteers eating horses because *"a horse rules the chariot."*[40] perhaps mirrored here in the idea of not sacrificing horses to a goddess connected to them.

Horses have long been seen as sacred animals in Ireland (O hOgain, 2006). Horses were a status symbol, a very practical means of transportation, work animals, and also served in warfare, the Irish fighting both mounted and with chariots. Horses often figure in mythological tales; for example, Cu Chulainn's horses played a role in the *Táin Bó Cúailgne,* including the Liath Macha [grey of Macha]; he acquired this magical steed after the horse emerged from the sidhe and the horse wept prophetic tears of blood before the hero's death. Holidays like Lughnasa, both in the distant and recent past, prominently featured horse racing, which might be a race over a flat course or involve the riders swimming the horses across a river. So significant was the social role of horses that from at least the medieval period even into modern times a horse might be kept as little more than a pet because of the prestige having such an animal gives to its owner (Patterson, 1994).

The horse was intrinsically linked to kingship and horse Goddesses seem almost invariably to be Goddesses of sovereignty as well. The symbolism of the horse as swift, brave, fertile, and intelligent are qualities reflected in the deities' horses were connected to (Green, 1991). A horse Goddess, ultimately, is a Goddess of sovereignty and the fertility of the land, who represents the land's ability to prosper and to be ruled well by the nobility.

Swords – A more obscure item connected to Macha is the sword. This comes from a reference in the *Táin Bó Cúailgne* where the sword is referred to as a sacred object of Macha:

> *"Fergus said: 'good men smile upon this and great deeds are made, by the point of my sword,* ***halidom of Macha,*** *swift vengeance [when] swords of the Leinstermen cry out.'"*.

A halidom is a sacred object, so this shows us that swords were viewed as sacred to Macha, and in the context of what Fergus is saying even possibly used to swear oaths.

Macha and Heads

One of the most significant associations Macha has – and often very underappreciated today – is to heads, specifically the severed heads or skulls of warriors. We see three separate references to this in the old glossaries:

> *"Macha, that is Badb or one of the three Morrigans, whence Macha's crop that is people's heads after the slaughter."*
>
> – O'Mulconry's Glossary

> *"Macha, that is Badb, one of the three Morrigans, that is Macha and Badb and Morrigan. Whence the crop of Macha, that is people's heads after the slaughter, having said that, dark red. Rough dwellings are over there. Where men sheer off Macha's crop, where warriors drive a multitude into pens, where the raven women cause battles."*
>
> – Irsan, Dublin, Trinity College,
> MS 1337 (H.3.18), pp. 79c–83b

> *"Macha, that is a crow or hooded crow, the heap of Macha that is collecting of a crow or a hooded crow."*
>
> – O'Clery's Glossary

The entry from *O'Mulconry's* is fairly straightforward and we see it repeated in the Irsan manuscript entry. Both use the word "mesrad" to describe the severed heads gathered as war trophies; mesrad is a general term for nuts often translated into English as masts. Mast is itself an archaic word for fallen nuts of any variety which were used to feed animals. This should create a pretty evocative image, of the severed heads of warriors being like the fallen nuts that cover the ground beneath trees, left to feed animals.

When we look at the, admittedly much later, entry in *O'Clery's Glossary* the nut reference has been lost entirely and instead

Macha is compared to "a crow or hooded crow"[41] and we are told that a "mol Macha", or heap, lump, or a rounded mass of Macha, is what is gathered or collected by crows, i.e. probably carrion although also possible heads. It is worth noting that the word mol used here is a form of mul and is used in compounds like mulcend which means round-headed and is closely related to mullach which is a term for the head, indicating at least a tenuous connection between this entry and the earlier ones. If we were to assume that *O'Clery's* is in fact a confusion of the earlier expressions we might see it more properly as "*the heads of Macha, that is what crows gather*" which is entirely logical and in line with the idiom. However, I can only speculate and as it stands the term used does literally mean heap or lump.

All three entries are clearly discussing Macha, although the first two give her the title of Badb[42] and describe her as one of the three Morrigans. The second entry makes it clear that calling her Badb is meant as a title as it is followed by listing her with Badb (as a separate being) as the three named Morrigans. The final entry does not mention the Morrigan or three Morrigans at all. The first two entries also clearly use what seemed to have been a well-known phrase "mesrad Mache" literally "masts of Macha" or "nut crop of Macha" and then explain that it is this which the severed heads of warriors are called. Based on this I think it is, at best, inaccurate to attribute the severed heads to the Morrigan either generally or specifically. They were clearly something associated with Macha in particular.

In the end what we have is three references to Macha and terms related to death. The first two refer to severed heads as her nut-crop; the second to what a crow gathers as her "heap" although I believe it's possible this is a later confusion of the earlier saying, given the similarity of the word used for heap with a related word for head. We know that severed heads were highly symbolic and meaningful in Irish culture and can safely assume that the connection between Macha and these heads is layered and significant. In all three cases we are given some beautiful, evocative imagery relating Macha to the trophies of war and to carrion.

Celtic culture in general, and the Irish in particular, were known to practice head hunting, the belief being that a person's power resided in their head. The heads of enemies would be taken with the belief that the owner of such a trophy would also possess the power of the person whose head was taken; in some cases, the head would be preserved, usually with oil, or else hung up for all to see as a trophy (Ross, 1998). The head was seen as the seat of the soul and repository of personal power. As Ross says:

> *"...a symbol which, in its way, sums up the whole of pagan Celtic religion... This is the symbol of the severed human head; in all its various modes of iconographic representation and verbal presentation, one may find the hard core of Celtic religion."* (Ross, 1998, p.154).

We see many references to heads being taken as trophies in the *Táin Bó Cúailgne* and find severed heads that talk and prophecy in other stories, reflecting the idea that the head retained its power after the person's death. Symbolic heads were also used and archaeologists have found examples of carved stone heads, which are believed to reflect the ideas associated with actual heads and skulls.

Macha in My Life – a Dream

I had a strange dream in 2014 about a ritual at Lughnasa. In the dream the people had gathered to honour Macha and Nuada at the harvest, which they were calling Brón Trogain. Everyone had met at a recently harvested field, the earth exposed with only a stubble of stems left jutting up in ragged rows. Two horses had been harnessed together with someone walking behind them, driving them. Two older girls walked in front and to each side of the horses, tossing handfuls of straw in their path. The horses were driven over the straw as someone prayed to Macha to bless the earth and Nuada to ward it. I do not remember all the words of the dream prayer, only this part – *"...walking, may your steps be sacred steps, walking, may Macha, raven of fierceness, bless this earth, walking, may Nuada, hound of battle, ward what we hold dear..."*.

When I woke up, I remembered the imagery and feeling of the dream quite vividly. I thought it was very odd because, although I know Brón Trogain is an alternate name for Lughnasa, it's not one I had ever used. Macha is tied to Lughnasa by the Oenacha (harvest fairs) at Emain Macha, but we don't have, as far as I know, any existing rituals or even hints of rituals for her at that time. Also, although there were traditions in the spring of leading horses over fresh planted fields to make the crops grow better (Ó'hÓgáin, *Lore of Ireland* mentions that) I don't know of any such rituals in the autumn.

I decided to do some research into the different parts of the dream and as expected didn't find anything relating to the ritual itself. Weirdly I did find a study showing the agricultural benefits of covering fields in cut straw over the winter, but I don't believe this was an Irish practice in antiquity. Macha is connected to horses, so the idea of the horses as a blessing agent had a certain logic to it. What I found most interesting though was looking up Brón Trogain in Old Irish. Usually, the name of the holiday is translated as *"sorrow of the earth"* because of the phrase given in the Wooing of Emer passage and it is firmly connected to the beginning of autumn and Lughnasa. I decided to look at what the words themselves actually meant to see if that could offer any insight. Brón means sorrow, grief, burden, or lamentation. Trogain not only means earth and autumn but also female raven, so it could be translated as "Sorrow of the (female) raven". Macha, of course, as one of the Morrigans is associated with both the hooded crow and the raven, forms that she was believed to take. Additionally, Trogan is associated with childbirth through this expression *"used as an imprecation [curse] troigh mhna troghuin foruibh `pangs of a woman in childbirth"* (eDIL, n.d.). I have long held the personal belief that it was at a Lughnasa aonach that Macha was forced to race the king's horses and gave birth to her twins, and cursed the men of Ulster, so the odd linguistic connections between the name Brón Trogain for the holiday and the translation of "sorrow of the raven", along with the connection of the word trogain, possibly, with a phrase relating to women in childbirth seems far from coincidental to me.

I still don't fully understand what this dream meant or why I had it. But I have personally been calling the holiday I celebrate on August 1st Brón Trogain since.

Chapter 7

Macha in the Modern World

"Badhbh Mácha ocus an Móirríoghan a dtrí baindée"
– Foras feasa ar Éirinn
Badb, Macha, and the Morrigan [were]
their three goddesses

In this final chapter we will be looking at various understandings of Macha in the 21st century, from appearances in media to common misunderstandings to ways you might connect to her today, if you are interested in doing so. This builds on everything we've discussed so far and offers both a view of her in the 21st century as well as options for those seeking to actively work with or honour this complex goddess.

Macha is not as present in modern media as the Morrigan herself is but she does make a few appearances, which I will discuss here. Looking at these kinds of media appearances can provide a deeper understanding of Macha and also show the ways that she is understood and depicted outside of pagan belief.

Macha in Fiction

The Hounds of the Morrigan by Pat O'Shae – Macha has a minor role in this novel, appearing as one of the Morrigan's sisters, who is in the guise of a motorcycle riding eccentric.

Sons of Macha – The third book in John Lenahan's young adult series is named for Macha. The series itself is about a teenage boy who discovers that he is from Tir na nÓg and has a series of adventures in and out of the human world.

The Secrets of the Immortal Nicholas Flamel by Michael Scott. A Young Adult book which features mythic beings and magic. Macha makes a minor appearance.

American Gods by Neil Gaiman.

The Conan series by Robert E Howard. Macha is part of the pantheon worshipped – or at least acknowledged – by the protagonist. Conan uses her name as an exclamation.

Marvel Comics – Macha appears as a character in the Marvel Earth-616 series where she is understood as a deity from an alternate dimension created by the primordial goddess Gaea. This version of Macha is the daughter of Danu and a character named Iorbonel, and with her sisters Morrigan and Badb forms a triad called 'the Morrigu', while with Badb and Nemain forms the triple goddess of Celtica. She is a war goddess and appears in stories mostly as a deity being invoked along with her sisters, particularly in the stories of Marvel's Doctor Druid.

Macha in Movies & TV

Song of the Sea – Macha is the name of the antagonist in this animated movie about a boy and his half-selkie sister. Known as the owl witch she is chasing down all Otherworldly beings on earth and turning them to stone, after first turning her own son into a mountain when his grief overwhelmed him. She sees this as a mercy, where she is removing people's feelings to keep them from feeling any pain or anguish. Called the 'Owl Witch' she appears as a very owl-like old woman.

Chilling Adventures of Sabrina – While Macha doesn't make an onscreen appearance in the show her name is invoked in a long list of female spirits to aid the witches in an exorcism spell. She is invoked along with Nemain and Badb, and in a wide group that includes goddesses, spirits, and famous human witches of the past.

Macha in Games

Macha appears in the role-playing game *Scion* produced by White Wolf. The premise of the game is that characters play the descendants of deities.

Common Misunderstandings About Macha

Although Macha is one of the Morrigans and the pre-eminent goddess of Ulster there are some significant misunderstandings about her, which in some cases radically change how people understand her. Below I will list the misinformation and then discuss the idea, hopefully helping to show where the truth may be.

She isn't one of the Morrigans – This idea is surprisingly common and one that I run across constantly, even in books. While some texts keep Macha in the group and place Nemain as the Morrigan's name, others exclude Macha and take Nemain in her place alongside Badb and the Morrigan. This is particularly odd because Macha is explicitly called one of the Morrigan in source material: "*Badb, Macha and Mórrígain are the three Mórrígna*" (Hennessy, 1870, p. 36) leaving little doubt about how she was historically understood. This may come from Macha strong connection as an individual goddess to Ulster or perhaps her less explicit connection to war in contrast to Nemain. Despite that though there is little doubt that Macha is one of the three Morrigans and was widely acknowledged as such across the sources.

She isn't a war goddess – Something I'm running across more often recently is the claim that Macha isn't a war goddess at all but only a sovereignty and fertility goddess. I suspect it may be rooted in the fact that of the three Morrigans Macha has perhaps the most complicated associations and the strongest overt connection to sovereignty. Despite this she is inarguably connected to war, particularly Macha of eth Tuatha De Danann and Macha Mongruadh who appear in their stories engaging in battle directly and, for Macha of the Tuatha De, with magic.

She's a crone goddess – This one can be found in both older pagan books and modern websites (likely drawing on the older books). For example, Edain McCoy's book *Witta* claims that Macha is interchangeable with the Cailleach and an aspect of the crone goddess; perhaps because of this people working within a maiden/mother/crone dynamic sometimes choose to place Macha as the crone. However – unlike the Morrigan and Badb – Macha never appears or is described as an older woman in any of her stories, she always appears as either a young woman or a woman in her prime. She is also distinct from the Cailleach with little to no overlap in their stories or folklore.

She isn't a goddess – This one is applied to Macha in particular and all the Irish gods in general, and does require some nuance to unpack especially with Macha. Because she has various appearances across myth and at least one of those is as a human character the argument is made that she is a deified human, that is a human who was turned into a goddess over time. In a wider sense some apply this argument to all of the Tuatha De Danann, seeing them as entirely deified human ancestors. Alternately some, like author Mark Williams, argue that all of the Irish gods, Macha inclusive, are literary creations constructed after the pagan period by Christian authors and commentators. This is a grey area which people will have their own views and opinions on but I think it's important to acknowledge she was called a goddess in some original texts, showing that at least in the medieval period she was understood to be a deity.

She is a goddess of childbirth – I've run into this a few times, even from an academic source. The idea is based on the story of Macha of the sidhe where she births twins, but that's literally the entire basis for it. There is nothing else in her stories to support the idea, and since she dies during childbirth or immediately after in some versions of that story, I'd personally be uncomfortable agreeing with it. For childbirth related things I'd look to Brighid.

The triple moon is her symbol – I've seen this claimed more widely for the Morrigan than Macha specifically but I wanted to include it anyway. People like this idea either because of the triple representation in the symbol or because it leans into Graves' Maiden/Mother/Crone paradigm, but it would be a very new idea.

Connecting to Macha as a Modern Pagan

For some people reading this book is likely only an academic exercise, a way to learn more about an intriguing deity, and that is entirely fair. For others though this book may represent an attempt to begin connecting to Macha or deepening an existing connection, and for those people I want to offer some possible methods to achieve those goals.

Altars and shrines are a great way to begin initially connecting to a deity and one of the first things I always suggest. My approach is to see an altar as an active place of worship and a shrine as a passive one, but I do acknowledge that the literal definitions of these terms are basically synonyms, so other people may not distinguish between them. In any case, you can begin by setting aside some space for her, decorated with things you associate with her or feel relate to her. At its simplest this might mean a picture of the mound at Emhain Macha or artwork representing her. If you have the space and feel motivated you can also make a more complex space perhaps with an altar cloth in her colours, imagery or statues of her or things you relate to her like horses, and tools including an offering plate or bowl, candles, and incense burner. The only real limits here are your available space and imagination.

My own altar to Macha features a cloth in a red and black Celtic knotwork pattern, a statue I have painted myself, candles, a small horse statue and small raven statue made of clay, an offering plate, and a bronze sword blessed to her. The statue was originally of a Welsh goddess and depicts a woman sitting on a throne nursing twins. I painted it based on my idea of Macha and use it to represent Macha of the Sidhe. When I am connecting to or honouring all three Morrigans I use three of Dryad Designs Morrigan statues together, with each painted differently to represent Macha, Badb, and the Morrigan.

Prayer can be an important and powerful way to feel connected to a deity or spirit. It is a way for you to speak to them and also to listen. Prayers can also bring a sense of support during troubled times and allow us to both honor a being and ask for certain types of help from them. They build connection, nurture a sense of belonging, and may give us a feeling of power when we are otherwise powerless. With that said I am offering here a small selection of prayers that I have written for Macha; I encourage people to write their own as well.

A prayer I wrote to Macha, for strength in difficult times, when I was struggling to stay strong as a parent caring for a chronically ill child:

"Macha, warrior, queen, goddess,
you were a mother too,
help me now to be strong

you ran against horses
while labouring and won;
let me find the strength to
endure my own race
Macha, help me be strong
Give me the courage
to keep running"

An invocation of Macha:

"I call to you, Red-haired Queen,
Lady of sovereignty
I call to you, Woman of the Sidhe,
Who runs swifter than any horse
I call to you, Battle Goddess,
Who gathers heads as trophies,
Fertile plain, racing mare, battle crow,
Macha, be with me now."

A prayer to Macha:

"Macha, Druidess of the Tuatha de Danann,
Skilled in magic, great in power, full in knowledge,
Guide my feet on my path, as I honour the old wisdom
Guide my hands in offering, as I honour the old Gods
Guide my heart in strength, as I honour the old ways."

Invocation to Macha:

Great Goddess, Mighty Macha,
Clearer of plains
Speaker of prophecy
Lady of the Holy People
I call to you

Warrior and Druidess
Wielder of fierce magic
Queen of the Tuatha De
I call to you
Sun of womanhood
Swifter than steeds
Lady of the Sidhe
I call to you
(each verse above could be used as a stand-alone with the first line if preferred)

Guided meditation to Meet Macha:

Relax and breathe deeply…in and out…in…and out…

Feel the solid earth beneath you. Let your spirit move down, out, into the earth. Fill yourself with the energy that rests deep in the soil…When you feel empowered by this energy pull your spirit back up, out of the earth.

You find yourself sitting on the ground at twilight. Next to you is a staff of Rowan carved with symbols. The ground is warm beneath you, but the air is starting to chill as darkness falls. There is a light wind and you can smell the scent of a fire somewhere in the distance and of fallen leaves close by. You hear the sounds of birds calling to each other as they settle in to roost for the night and the murmuring of water over rocks. Although it is deep twilight and the world around you is dark you can see clearly. You are sitting in a field between an old forest and a river. At the other end of the field the shape of a hill rises up, a gentle curve in the earth.

As you look at the hill something catches your eye, flickering like firelight. You stand up, pick up the staff, and move towards the light… as you walk across the field towards the hill the light grows. As you get closer you can see that the light is coming from a door that opens up into the hill midway up the incline. Using the staff to help, you climb up the hill to the door.

At the entrance to the hollow hill you meet a guide who greets you and welcomes you into the hill, leading you through the doorway and into the hill. You step through into an open expanse of grass with a forest at its edge. You walk towards the woods and enter beneath the trees following a wide path. Your guide leads you on and on, until you reach a small clearing.

Your guide gestures you forward and as you cross into the open space a figure emerges from the far side. She is beautiful, her red hair tumbling around her shoulders, dressed as a warrior and bearing a sword at her side. She watches you with an amused expression to see what you will do next. You bow your head slightly as a sign of respect and then greet Macha.

(take time here to experience whatever occurs and let the experience unfold organically)

When you have done what you need to do your Guide gently tells you it is time to leave. You bow to the goddess again and then step back carefully into the trees, turning to make your way back through the woods. The path leads you back, twisting and turning, the trees close on each side. Finally, the greenwood path opens up into the wild field you first crossed and you cross it again to return back to the hill you started from. Your Guide leads you back through the hill and hall to the entrance you arrived at.

At the entrance you say farewell to your Guide before stepping out the door. As you do the door closes and the doorway vanishes into the hill. You are standing alone on the now in the dark night. Carefully you climb down the hill and walk back across the field. The night is silent now, and dark, and the wind is cold. Put down the staff and sit down, resting on the earth.

Feel the solid earth beneath you. Let your spirit move down, out, into the earth. Fill yourself with the energy that rests deep in the soil…When you feel empowered by this energy pull your spirit back up, out of the earth.

Return to your body; feel yourself solidly back in mortal earth.

Relax and breathe deeply… in…and out…in and out…

Move slowly, reconnecting to your body, until you are ready to open your eyes.

Write down everything you saw or experienced in your journal.

Macha in My Life – Macha's Sword

I dedicated myself as a priestess of Macha in roughly the mid 2000's, as she had been a strong presence in my life for a long time prior to that. For several years after that dedication, I knew that I needed to find a bronze sword for ritual use, but I never felt a huge need to get it done, just a general sense that eventually it would be needed. In late 2013 that sense started to become more urgent, and I realized why after finding out that I had to have a sword for a ritual I had volunteered to participate in at the first Morrigan's Call Retreat. I cannot work with iron so finding a bronze blade became a top priority and complicated the quest. This is the story of Macha's sword and how I came into possession of it.

I knew that the only realistic option would be to commission the sword and several people recommended that I check out Neil Burridge's website because he specifically works with bronze and does make blades on commission. His selection is good and the quality was vouched for by multiple people so I decided to email him. Because he offers replicas of blades found in Britain and I was looking for an Irish blade I requested the closest sword in style to what I wanted. I was pleasantly surprised when the sword maker contacted me and opened a dialogue offering an opportunity for me to explain exactly what I was looking for, and even more pleasantly surprised when he offered another option, a slight variation on one of his stock swords. This blade was very similar, he said, to an archaeological find from the Nooan area of Inchiquin in Ireland and he provided a link with some information. The find was associated with Lake Inchiquin, itself a place rich in fairy lore, and I was pretty quickly won over to the idea.

This all occurred around Imbolc of 2014 and I knew I needed to get the blade within a few months; however, I was forewarned that the actual forging might take some time. Things proceeded faster than expected though and I was contacted again on the 14th of that same month and told that the blade had been cast. That day, Cornwall, where the sword was being made, was experiencing severe storms similar to what in the United States would be called a hurricane and it was in the midst of this storm and its immediate aftermath that the sword was made. It seemed entirely appropriate that this sword, intended to be dedicated to Macha, was born in a storm with all that energy around it.

It also came about that the sword was blessed by its makers at a holy well in Cornwall, the Madron Well. Triple blessed, actually, being taken to a clootie tree at the site as well as laid on the stones of the well itself and dipped in the waters. I felt extremely lucky and honored that this was able to be done for the blade, but somehow also not surprised; at this point it was clear that the sword wasn't an ordinary commissioned piece. It had a spirit of its own already and a sacredness to it.

After being forged, hilted and blessed it was duly packaged and began its journey across the ocean. This was a rather nerve-wracking process, as it ended up being held in customs for several weeks, and the idea of it being lost in transit was rather appalling as it could never have truly been replaced. But finally, a few days shy of the spring equinox, it arrived safely. (I'll add here – if you ever order a sword from over-seas anticipate it being held in customs and be prepared for a longer wait time. Expecting the delay won't make it any less stressful, but at least you'll know it takes longer than usual).

The blade was blessed here and dedicated to Macha on the equinox. It travelled with me to the Morrigan Retreat in June of 2014 (and many subsequent years as well) and played its part in a ritual for Her – and truly has proved to be a sacred thing of Hers. It rests near Her statue and devotional items on my altar now, until it is needed again.

Conclusion

> *"The furies and monsters and hags of doom cried aloud so that their voices were heard in the rocks and waterfalls and in the hollows of the earth…. In the van of the Tuatha De advanced the [warriors and] the three queens, Ere, Fotla and Banba, and the three sorceresses, Badb, Macha and the Morigan, with Bechuille and Danann their two foster-mothers. They fixed their pillars in the ground to prevent any one fleeing till the stones should flee."*
>
> – The First Battle of Moytirra, Fraser, 1916

Macha is a complex goddess, as we have seen throughout this book. She appears in stories as a primal being, a creatrix, a war goddess, a woman of the Sidhe, and a human queen, with each version ambiguously related to the others leaving a lot of room for debate and personal belief. However, when we look closely at each of these appearances, we can find threads that connect them, deeper themes and purviews that they share, and story motifs that echo each other. Each story can be read and understood separately, taken as a cohesive whole, or stitched together from specific pieces, yet Macha remains the driving force behind them. She is different in each yet also the same, in a contradiction that is foundational to understanding her. Macha is more than the sum of her individual stories; she is a constant presence throughout the wider story of Irish myth and is solidly anchored in the modern world, embedded in the land and living within the human heart.

This book hasn't been about dictating to the reader what to believe about Macha, but rather about offering the mythology and modern ideas so that the reader can decide for themselves. No one can tell you what you believe or how this information will make sense to you, and as shown in the introduction even scholars don't agree on these things. Macha, no matter how well we know her, is a mystery who defies precise definitions. Her strength lies in that fact, in her inability to be easily understood or reduced down to a simple view. There is no right or wrong in how you as an individual conceptualize Macha or how you believe her stories join together – or don't. Even after decades of studying her, honouring her, and acting as her priestess I still question things and work – and re-work – these pieces together in new combinations.

In many ways the wider story of Macha is the story of the Tuatha De Danann because they also are more complex and convoluted than they first appear. Across history and into today people have endlessly debated who and what the Tuatha De are, what role they played in pagan Ireland, if they existed as gods there, and how people would have understood them in the past. Were they literary inventions of the Middle Ages? Were they ancestral spirits? Were they gods imported from continental Celtic cultures or were they born in Ireland? Each of these questions has been asked of the Tuatha De and also of Macha herself as various writers wrestle with her stories and try to find cohesive answers to her place in myth and in human belief.

At the start of this text, I said that when people hear or see Macha's name, they often immediately think of the Morrigan, subsuming her as an individual into the grouping she is part of with her sisters. I hope that this book has shown that Macha is much more than just one of the three Morrigans, that she is a force in her own right and a powerful deity with a distinct personality. She is one of the Morrigans but she isn't only that, and her connection to her sisters offers just one small piece of her to those seeking. As powerful and important as that role is for her, and it is an essential aspect of Macha, she isn't limited to or by the title Morrigan, rather it forms a foundation that is built on from there. In the same way that she is a battle goddess but also more than just a battle goddess, she is one of the Great Queens but also much more than just one face of the Morrigan. Understanding her means looking beyond the surface and beyond the Morrigan to find the depth of the individual within the group.

Macha is the wife of Partholón who helped to settle Ireland and bring civilization to the wilderness. She is the wife of Nemed who shaped the land and foresaw the distant future. She is one of the Morrigans who with her sisters brought battle magic and victory to the Tuatha De Danann. She is the fairy woman who cursed the men of Ulster for their cruelty to her and set the stage for the greatest Irish epic, the Cattle Raid of Cooley. She is the human queen who wouldn't accept her place being limited by powerful men and who ruled by her own might. She is all of these things, and she is more than these things. Her stories are a beginning to understanding her, not an end, just as the myths are a beginning to understanding the Irish gods but not an end.

The Dindshenchas calls Macha 'the sun of womanhood'; may she light your way as you seek to understand her through the complex layers of story that surround her.

Appendix A

Pronunciation Guide

This is the usual Appendix where I suggest some ways to pronounce some names and some terms found within this book. I don't use IPA but will offer some basic phonetic options. I hope this can help readers get an idea of how these names might sound, with an understanding that there are dialect variations beyond this. As always, I encourage people to go to Irish speakers, if possible, for anything related to the Irish language.

Badb – bive or bave
Macha – Mah-(k)uh, with the ch like in loch
Liath Macha – Lee-uh Mah-(k)uh
Cu Chulainn – Koo Hu-lahn
Crunnchu – Krun-(k)u
Nuada – Noo-uh-thuh
Nemed – Neh-ved
Lúnasa – Loo-nuh-suh
Tuatha De Danann – Too-uh-huh Day dah-nann
Fir Bolg – Fehr Bol-ihg
Sidhe – shee
Aos Sidhe – ace shee
Emain Macha – eh-wen Mah(k)uh
Fír – feer
Fial – fe-uhl
Cimbaeth – Kihm-bay(th)
Aedh – Ay
Rua – Roo-ah
Dithorba – Dih-(th)uhr-buh

Appendix B

Story Sources and Recommended Resources

Macha appears across a range of myths and for readers who want to look at her stories in these sources I'd like to offer a short list of places to start:

The Lebor Gabala Erenn – The Book of Invasions of Ireland
Cét-Cath Maige Tuired – First Battle of Moytirra
Cath Maige Tuired – Battle of Moytirra
Ulster Cycle – particularly the Noinden Ulaid, the Debility of the Ulstermen
Dindshenchas – lore of places
Banshenchas – lore of women
Sanas Cormaic – Cormac's Glossary
Foras feasa ar Erinn – the history of Ireland

In addition to those primary sources, I'd also like to include a wider list of sources on the Morrigan in general which also often include or apply to Macha.

Dissertations and Papers

There are some great academic works out there on the Morrigan which include Macha. There are also some that I don't entirely agree with but still recommend because they add important layers to any discussion about the Morrigan and deities related to Her.

War-goddesses, furies and scald crows: The use of the word badb in early Irish literature by Kim Heidja
The 'Mast' of Macha: The Celtic Irish and the War Goddess of Ireland by Catherine Mowat

War Goddess: The Morrigan and Her Germano-Celtic Counterparts by Angelique Gulermovich Epstein

Demonology, allegory and translation: the Furies and the Morrigan by Michael Clarke

The 'Terror of the Night' and the Morrígain: Shifting Faces of the Supernatural by Jacqueline Borsje

Macha and the Invention of Myth by Gregory Toner, Éiru, Volume 60

Tochmarc Cruinn Ocus Macha [the wooing of Cruinn and Macha] by Thurneysen in Zeitschrift für Celtische Philologie [Note: Text is in German]

Playing for Power: Macha Mongrúad's Sovereign Performance by Amy Sheehan in Constructing Gender in Medieval Ireland. The New Middle Ages

The One Who Is Many, The Many Who Are One: Power and Potentiality in the Sacred Females of Pre-Christian Ireland by S Rowley

Macha and Conall Cernach: A study of two iconographic patterns in medieval Irish narratives and Celtic art by Paula Coe

Books

To the best of my current knowledge this book is itself the first attempt at a text entirely dedicated to and focused on Macha. That said for readers looking to go deeper in a pagan framework there are a few books I would suggest which are about the Morrigan more generally but will include bits about Macha.

The Morrigan, Ireland's Goddess: Sovereign Secrets from an Irish View by Lora O'Brien

The Book of The Great Queen: The Many Faces of the Morrigan from Ancient Legends to Modern Devotions by Morpheus Ravenna

Celtic Lore and Spellcraft of the Dark Goddess by Stephanie Woodfield

The Morrigan by Courtney Weber

Websites

An assortment of Morrigan related websites out there that I am aware of and whose content is generally reliable and will touch on Macha:

Scath na Feannoige – Morrigan content and content focused on the warrior path. Some free and some paid access, but excellent material.

Mary Jones Celtic Literature Collective – As advertised, a resource for all things Celtic. your best source for myths on Macha (in the Irish lit section) and also offering an encyclopaedia section. The myths suggested above can be found in English translations at this site.

Story Archaeology – A great resource for newer translations of the myths and discussion of the stories in context. if you search the site/podcast you'll find results relating to Macha.

Coru Cathubodua – A site by a group dedicated to the Morrigan, with articles and a resource list including content on Macha.

Artwork

Some of my personal favourite examples of Morrigan artwork:

"Macha Curses the Men of Ulster" by Stephen Reid 1904

"Macha the Irish goddess of war" by Jeremy McHugh

"MÓR-RÍOGHAIN" by Jane Brideson (technically of the Morrigan but shows all three sisters)

Additionally, artist Naomi Cornock has several intense images of Macha

Endnotes

1. Cumal or cumhal is also a term for a female slave.
2. The Fomorians are a mysterious group with no known origins in myths who often act as antagonists in stories. The name is of uncertain meaning but may be related to the sea or ocean, and the Fomorians represent a primordial power. This will be discussed in slightly more depth in the next chapter.
3. Although there have been attempts to approach the various invasions of Ireland as historic events tied to known cultures, I will be taking the mythology here at face value as mythology and approaching these various groups as spirit peoples rather than humans.
4. We do not necessarily have manuscripts which have survived from the earlier dating periods but we have later copies of those manuscripts which can be dated to those periods based on the language and style used.
5. I will offer a retelling of this story in Chapter 4.
6. Fo – under, mara – the sea or ocean.
7. Alternately according to the *Dindshenchas* 26 plains.
8. Alternately 12 days, according to the *Annals of the Four Masters*.
9. Samhain was a traditional time to pay rent, and remained so through the early modern period.
10. Alternately I will note this may be an artifact of different regional variations of stories being woven together, creating contradictions in the narrative.
11. Tuatha De [people of the Gods] is the older term. Tuatha De Danann [people of the goddess Danu or people of the gods of skill] is a later version used by Christian scribes to differentiate from the biblical use of Tuatha De as 'people

of God' used for the Israelites in the old Testament. I will be using both forms here.

12. The Christian scribes recording this story in the *Lebor Gabala Erenn* explain away the mystical elements by following this passage with an insertion which claims the Tuatha De arrived in wooden ships at the shore then burnt their ships creating smoke which covered the land.
13. It is unclear who exactly this figure is; it is possible this is Danu but it may also be a misspelling of Dinann, a daughter of Flidais. This second theory is somewhat supported by a later passage in which Danann and Be Chuille – a daughter of Flidais – are named as the foster mothers of the three Morrigans.
14. Hence the name of the story: 'maig tuired' means plain of pillars.
15. 1 November.
16. This translation is my own; other translators may handle some of this passage differently, particularly 'that is a crow' which may also be read as 'that is Badb' and the final line about raven women stirring up strife, as the phrase mna trogain is used idiomatically elsewhere for childbirth but I am giving it literally here.
17. Along with a range of sub-groups.
18. This gives us Nuada's most well-known epithet argatlam, meaning silver arm.
19. I have always personally strongly associated Macha and the colour red, which is probably part of why I saw her this way.
20. The version of the story I am offering here combines material found in the *Metrical Dindshenchas*, the *Edinburgh Dindshenchas*, and the *Rennes Dindshenchas* as well as the *Noínden Ulaid* from the *Ulster Cycle*.
21. An oenach – an assembly or gathering much like a modern harvest fair, with games, tests of skill, and sales.
22. This was something of a cultural taboo at the time.

23. She was asking for this not only to avoid racing until after she'd delivered but also because being seen publicly in such a state violated social rules of the time, denying her privacy and modesty in front of strangers. Denying a woman such modesty was believed to weaken men (Waddell, 2014).
24. Alternately nine days and nights.
25. Either because he was too young or because he wasn't born in Ulster.
26. Alternate versions say that Macha died.
27. The meaning of Emhain is uncertain. In this case the story is claiming it is a form of emon, a term for multiple children born together.
28. This is at Navan Centre and Fort, accessible to the public and open for tours. The Centre offers accommodations for autistic patrons on request. There are also links on the website for a virtual tour in pictures. Information can be found here https://visitarmagh.com/places-to-explore/navan-centre-fort/
29. I'm not going to get into the debate about when exactly Samhain occurs here. There are several competing theories. For my purpose here its being viewed through the historic date of 1 November, although I would argue it is a period of time not a specific date.
30. As with the previous chapter I am offering an amalgamated version of Macha Mongruadh's story which combines the key points of several *Dindshenchas* tales.
31. Fadó, fadó, in Éirinn...
32. Aedh Rua means red fire, but Aedh is a fairly common man's name in older Irish material. He is described as having red hair and his name may also be read as Aedh of the Red (Hair).
33. This offers an alternate if more dubious origin of the fort's name from the one given in the last chapter.

34. Red is often associated with Otherworldly beings in Irish myth and folklore, usually the more dangerous types.
35. A fish in Irish mythology which contained great wisdom because it fed on the hazelnuts falling from trees of knowledge around the pool. To eat the salmon was to absorb that wisdom.
36. Discussed in a previous chapter.
37. An Irish term which encompasses sovereignty, the right to rule, but also means a kingdom; Macha gives the right to rule but also the kingdom itself.
38. A similar pattern of building and burning occurred at the other two large ritual sites in Ireland: Dún Ailinne and Teamhair.
39. This is the older Irish name. In modern Irish they would be called Aonach (plural Aonachaigh).
40. Tochmarc Emire.
41. It is possibly that this entry should be read as "Macha, that is Badb, or a hooded crow. However, since the second line would then have to be read very awkwardly as "a collection of Badb's or a hooded crow" it seems more likely to me that O'Clery intended badb in the sense of a crow. The reader may conclude otherwise.
    Also there's a fun play on words here, as mol and cruinn (the root of cruinnuighadh) both mean rounded lump
42. Badb, like Morrigan, is both a personal name and a title applied to similar beings.

Bibliography

Anderson, G., (2008) *Birds in Ireland: Facts, Folklore, and History*

Briggs, K., (1976) *A Dictionary of Fairies*

Carey, J., (1981) "The Name 'Tuatha Dé Danann'" Éigse, Vol. 18, prt. 2

—— (1983) "Notes on the Irish War-Goddess" Éigse, Vol. 19, prt. 2,

Clark, R., (1991) *The Great Queens: Irish Goddesses from the Morrigan to Cathleen ní Hoolihan*

Coe, P., (1995) "Macha and Conall Cernach: A Study of Two Iconographic Patterns in Medieval Irish Narratives and Celtic Art" [dissertation]

Dobbs, M., (1930) *The Ban-Shenchus; Revue Celtique*, vol 47

—— (1932) *"The Ban-shenchus". Revue Celtique* vol 49

eDIL (2024) Electronic Dictionary of the Irish Language

Fraser, J., (1916) "The First Battle of Moytura." Ériu v.8

Freeman, P., (2002) *War, Women, and Druids*

Giles, J., (2000) *Historia Brittonum*

Green, M., (1992) *Dictionary of Celtic Myth and Legend*

—— (1992) *Animals in Celtic Life and Myth*

—— (1995) *Celtic Goddesses*

Grey, E., (1983) *Cath Maige Tuired*

Gulermovich Epstein, A., (1998) "War goddess: the Morrígan and her Germano-Celtic counterparts" [dissertation]

Gwynn, E., (1924) *Metrical Dindshenchas* vol 4

Heijda, K., (2007) "War-goddesses, furies and scald crows: The use of the word badb in early Irish literature" [thesis]

Hennessey, W., (1870) *Ancient Irish Goddess of War*

House of Apples (2025) Macha's Justice, retrieved from https://houseofapples.org/machasjustice

Keating, G., (1914) Foras Feasa ar Eirinn

Macalister, R., (1944) *Lebor Gabala Erenn* vol 4

MacCana, P., (1970) *Celtic Mythology*

Maiche (n.d.) Sanas Cormac. Retrieved from http://www.asnc.cam.ac.uk/irishglossaries/search.php?sText=Maiche

McCormick, F., (2009) 'Ritual feasting in Iron Age Ireland'. In Relics of Old Decency: Archaeological Studies in Later Prehistory. Retrieved from https://pure.qub.ac.uk/en/publications/ritual-feasting-in-iron-age-ireland

McNeill, M., (1962) *The Festival of Lughnasa*

Meyer, K., (1890) *The Wooing of Emer*

—— (1907) 'The Dindshenchas of Emain Macha'; Archiv für Celtische Lexikographie

Monaghan, P., (2004) *Encyclopedia of Celtic Mythology and Folklore*

Ó Crualaoich, G., (2003) *The Book of the Cailleach*

O'Curry, E,. (1861) Lectures on the manuscript materials of ancient Irish history Dublin. Retrieved from https://www.maryjones.us/ctexts/macha.html

O'Donovan, J., (1848) *Annals of the Kingdom of Ireland by the Four Masters*

O'Grady, S., (1892) *Silva Gadelica*

Ó'hÓgáin, D., (1995) *Irish Superstitions*

—— (2006) *The Lore of Ireland*

Patterson, N., (1994) *Cattle Lords and Clansmen; The social structure of early Ireland*

Puuvel, J., (1981) "Aspects of Equine Functionality," in Analecta Indoeuropaea

Ross, A., (1998) *Pagan Celts*

Russell, P., Moran, P., Arbuthnot, S., (2023) Early Irish Glossaries Database, version 3.3 Retrieved from www.asnc.cam.ac.uk/irishglossaries/

Sherwood, A., (2009) *An Bó Bheannaithe: Cattle Symbolism in Traditional Irish Folklore, Myth, and Archaeology*

Sjoestedt, M., (2000) *Celtic Gods and Heroes*

Smyth, D., (1988) *A Guide to Irish Mythology*

Stokes, W., (1893) 'The Edinburgh Dindshenchas', Folklore 4

Toner, G., (2010) "Macha and the Invention of Myth". Ériu. V.60
Waddell, J., (2014) *Archaeology and Celtic Myth*
Williams, M., (2016) *Ireland's Immortals*

About the Author

Morgan Daimler is a witch who has been a polytheist since the early '90s. Following a path inspired by the Irish Fairy Faith blended with neopagan witchcraft. Morgan teaches classes on Irish myth and magical practices, fairies, and related subjects in the United States and internationally. Morgan has been published in multiple anthologies as well as in Witches and Pagans magazine, and Pagan Dawn magazine, and she is one of the world's foremost experts on all things Fairy.

SELECTED TITLES

Irish Mythology
Lugh
The Dagda
The Morrigan
Irish Paganism
Raven Goddess
Manannán mac Lir
Pantheon: The Irish

Tales of the Tuatha De Danann, Volume 1
Tales of the Tuatha De Danann, Volume 2
(New Translations of Irish Myths)

Fairy Lore
Fairies
Fairycraft
Aos Sidhe
Fairy Witchcraft
21st Century Fairy
A New Dictionary of Fairies

MOON BOOKS

PAGANISM & SHAMANISM

What is Paganism? A religion, a spirituality, an alternative belief system, nature worship? You can find support for all these definitions (and many more) in dictionaries, encyclopaedias, and text books of religion, but subscribe to any one and the truth will evade you. Above all Paganism is a creative pursuit, an encounter with reality, an exploration of meaning and an expression of the soul. Druids, Heathens, Wiccans and others, all contribute their insights and literary riches to the Pagan tradition. Moon Books invites you to begin or to deepen your own encounter, right here, right now.

If you have enjoyed this book, why not tell other readers by posting a review on your preferred book site.

Bestsellers from Moon Books
Pagan Portals Series

The Morrigan

Meeting the Great Queens

Morgan Daimler

Ancient and enigmatic, the Morrigan reaches out to us. On shadowed wings and in raven's call, meet the ancient Irish goddess of war, battle, prophecy, death, sovereignty, and magic.

Paperback: 978-1-78279-833-0 ebook: 978-1-78279-834-7

The Awen Alone

Walking the Path of the Solitary Druid

Joanna van der Hoeven

An introductory guide for the solitary Druid, The Awen Alone will accompany you as you explore, and seek out your own place within the natural world.

Paperback: 978-1-78279-547-6 ebook: 978-1-78279-546-9

Moon Magic

Rachel Patterson

An introduction to working with the phases of the Moon, what they are and how to live in harmony with the lunar year and to utilise all the magical powers it provides.

Paperback: 978-1-78279-281-9 ebook: 978-1-78279-282-6

Hekate

A Devotional

Vivienne Moss

Hekate, Queen of Witches and the Shadow-Lands, haunts the pages of this devotional bringing magic and enchantment into your lives.

Paperback: 978-1-78535-161-7 ebook: 978-1-78535-162-4

Bestsellers from Moon Books

Keeping Her Keys

An Introduction to Hekate's Modern Witchcraft

Cyndi Brannen

Blending Hekate, witchcraft and personal development together to create a powerful new magickal perspective.

Paperback: 978-1-78904-075-3 ebook 978-1-78904-076-0

Journey to the Dark Goddess

How to Return to Your Soul

Jane Meredith

Discover the powerful secrets of the Dark Goddess and transform your depression, grief and pain into healing and integration.

Paperback: 978-1-84694-677-6 ebook: 978-1-78099-223-5

Shamanic Reiki

Expanded Ways of Working with Universal Life Force Energy

Llyn Roberts, Robert Levy

Shamanism and Reiki are each powerful ways of healing; together, their power multiplies. Shamanic Reiki introduces techniques to help healers and Reiki practitioners tap ancient healing wisdom.

Paperback: 978-1-84694-037-8 ebook: 978-1-84694-650-9

Southern Cunning

Folkloric Witchcraft in the American South

Aaron Oberon

Modern witchcraft with a Southern flair, this book is a journey through the folklore of the American South and a look at the power these stories hold for modern witches.

Paperback: 978-1-78904-196-5 ebook: 978-1-78904-197-2